**SCHOLASTIC**

# Fluency Strategies
# for Struggling Readers

Marcia Delany

New York • Toronto • London • Auckland • Sydney
Mexico City • New Delhi • Hong Kong • Buenos Aires

Teaching
*Resources*

*My sincere thanks to the following people:*

*Thelma Dill and Laura Toburen, former principals of
Washington-Wilkes Primary School, who supported and
encouraged me in my efforts to reach struggling readers*

*The teachers, administrators, staff, and students at
Washington-Wilkes Primary School and the many other
teachers and students with whom I have worked*

*My editor, Sarah Longhi, who has guided
me with expertise and endless patience
through the publication process*

*A very special thanks to my husband, Jack,
without whose unfailing love and support
I would not have been able to write this book.*

Cover design by Victor Zarkovic
Interior design by Kelli Thompson
Interior photos by Marcia Delany
ISBN: 0-439-60970-4

3 4 5 6 7 8 9 10      40      12 11 10 09 08 07

# Contents

# Introduction

In the summer of 2005, while I was shopping in Atlanta, I ran into Alicia, one of my former first graders. I was absolutely delighted to see her and to hear that she was finishing a bachelor's degree at a state university. This came as a particularly satisfying discovery for me, her first reading teacher.

When I met her, Alicia was reading below grade level and came to me for two hours every day for extra reading support. She was a bright child who was very enthusiastic about learning to read, but she needed a lot of support to gain grade-level fluency. Her knowledge of letter sounds was limited and she recognized only a few sight words. Given a short passage with basic words she knew, she read word-by-word at a very slow rate, which sounded labored and monotonous. She did not read to comprehend—she read to get through the text at hand.

To help Alicia become a fluent reader who found meaning and enjoyment in what she read, I employed many of the fluency strategies described in this book. I used strategies that would increase her decoding and word recognition skills as well as her phrasing and expression. As Alicia's confidence grew, she not only began to read more smoothly and rapidly, she also began to keep her own box of favorite books and enjoyed going back to practice her favorites and perform them for me and her family. She was becoming a fluent reader. By the end of her first-grade school year, Alicia was reading and comprehending at grade level. Seven years later she had earned a place in the top eighth-grade language arts class at the middle school. And now, in her young adulthood, college graduation is on the horizon.

**W**hile oral reading skills alone did not create Alicia's success story, they have laid a strong foundation for her academic growth and that of many of her struggling reader peers.

Improving fluency has been a part of my teaching agenda for more than 36 years. Much of what I've learned about how to help children improve their reading was learned through continuing coursework, the work of leading educators and researchers on fluency, and, most important, through working with children like Alicia. My work has shown me that with a supportive teacher, good assessment, and repeated encounters with reading materials in ways that target a child's fluency needs, struggling readers can become fluent readers—and success stories.

## *About This Book*

**U**nlike other fluency books geared to teachers of this age group, this book focuses specifically on struggling readers. It provides a brief overview of oral reading fluency including what it is and why being a fluent oral reader is so important to reading for comprehension. Most importantly, this book provides you with ways to develop children's oral reading fluency through a variety of engaging strategies and activities that you can easily make a part of your everyday instruction—either with the whole class, small groups, or individuals.

The 20 fluency strategies included in this book are presented in a lesson format through the use of individual student vignettes and step-by-step, easy-to-follow procedures. In each lesson, you'll find an approach that incorporates the following fluency instruction principles based on the work of reading experts Timothy Rasinski and Jay Samuels.

Students need:

- multiple opportunities to hear the fluent reading of text (Rasinski, 2003b)

- practice through repeated oral readings of a text (Samuels, 1979)

- guidance in their reading practice (Rasinski, 2003a)

The strategy lessons are designed to develop children's fluency through the use of texts and materials that you already have or can create with minimal preparation in your classroom. In each lesson, a section titled Putting It to Work in Your Classroom provides four steps for implementation: Preparing and Introducing the Activity; Modeling Fluent Oral Reading; Guiding Repeated Oral Reading; and Extending Repeated Oral Reading, which includes engaging activities that extend the learning in the lesson.

The strategies are organized by chapter to address the specific fluency issues of accuracy and automaticity (chapters 1, 2, and 3) and phrasing, expression, and prosody (chapters 3 and 4). Although oral reading rate is a component of fluency, I do not offer strategies that specifically target rate improvement. This is because a child's reading rate increases as his or her accuracy, automaticity, phrasing, expression, and prosody increase—gains that can be made by lots of reading practice supported by the lessons in this book. Chapter 5 describes types of fluency assessments and gives you the tools you need to evaluate your struggling readers and effectively plan instruction that meets their needs.

## *How to Use This Book*

First, take some time to familiarize yourself with the fluency terms and definitions you'll encounter in the chapters ahead (see pages 8–10). Determine which of your readers are in need of fluency-targeted instruction and determine their areas of challenge. You may already have assessment data that indicates students' specific needs, or you may want to use the fluency assessment procedures and tools in Chapter 5. Then use the chart on page 11 to find strategy lessons that address the specific fluency needs of your readers. The symbols shown in the chart serve as a quick reference to help you find lessons that address particular needs. Use the lessons as guidelines and add your own innovations: You may wish to adapt a given lesson to meet the specific needs and interests of your children. Remember to keep the activities quick and fun, and have children return to meaningful text to practice new skills as much as possible.

### LESSON MATERIALS

I find the following materials useful when teaching the lessons in this book. Some are simple to make, others are tools that your school may have on hand.

- **Word cards and letter cards.** I use 4" x 6" index cards and markers to make word cards and letter cards. Manipulating the cards encourages children to practice working with letters, sounds, and sight or vocabulary words. For example, some of the lessons suggest that children use letter or word cards to build words and sentences. You may wish to laminate the cards you create for durability.

> The strategies in this book provide your struggling readers with multiple opportunities to hear fluent expressive oral reading and to engage in the repeated reading of words, phrases, sentences, and text. This repeated exposure and practice is a key element to making gains in reading achievement.

- **Rings.** I use metal rings to hang chart paper with word lists and to make letter and sight-word mini–flip charts. Punching a hole at the top of each word card and then grouping similar cards (short vowels or word families) together and attaching them with a ring enables you to create a manipulative that the child can use by flipping through the cards on the ring. This becomes a helpful tool for children to use independently or with a partner for practicing and reinforcing their recognition of letters and sight words.

- **Magnetic letters, magnetic boards, and letter tiles.** I use magnetic letters and letter tiles to give children an alternative to word and letter cards. Their color and form often help tactile and visual learners remember the shape of each letter more accurately. You might want to have the children place the magnetic letters on individual magnetic boards or right on a table or desk.

- **Small whiteboard.** I use a small dry-erase board when I work with individuals and small groups of children. This portable tool can be adjusted so that everyone in the group can easily see it. As suggested in several of the strategy lessons, I write familiar words featuring key letters or sounds and write sentences that the children and I create together. When I want to highlight an element, I can do so with markers of different colors. I can also have children come to the board to write a letter or fill in missing letters, or to write the words they are learning.

- **Pocket charts.** I find pocket charts very useful when I have children work with letter and word cards and sentences. For example, the words we use to build different sentences can be mixed up and placed in the pocket chart. I might have children build the sentences in the pocket chart during center time.

- **Large whiteboard or chalkboard.** I use a large board for writing longer text such as lists of multisyllabic words or the writing of a child's dictated experience story.

- **Teacher-made checklists.** I make my own checklists (they are part of my lesson plan) when I teach letter, sound, and word recognition. Checklists enable you to be sure that individual children have mastered the material and to identify areas where they need more support.

- **Chart paper.** I use chart paper for listing the words, rhymes, and poems we work with in the classroom. I generally hang the pages on a chart stand or tape them to a wall or board where children can use them for reference.

# Fluency Terms and Definitions

The terms below include key concepts that you will likely encounter as you read this and other resources about oral reading fluency.

**accuracy:** the correct identification of words; reading without substituting, mispronouncing, or omitting the words in the text

**appropriate reading rate:** reading at an oral rate that is grade-level appropriate and varying the reading rate according to the purpose for reading

**automaticity:** processing text rapidly and with little attention or effort; having no difficulty recognizing words and decoding words in text at or above the reader's grade level

**choppy phrasing:** grouping words inappropriately, without attention to meaning; may indicate a lack of comprehension

> **Example:** A disfluent reader may phrase the sentence *The girl and the boy want to visit their grandma* in this way:
>
> *The / girl and / the / boy want / to visit their / grandma.*

**decoding:** sounding out the parts or syllables of a word for the purpose of determining its intended meaning

**expression:** appropriate phrasing and prosody that make oral reading sound like spoken language

**grade-level text:** level of reading difficulty determined by publishers or teachers using a readability formula, so that the text reflects only the words and features of a text appropriate for a given grade level

**guided practice:** teacher-supported reading and rereading of words or text for fluency

**hesitation:** a pause while reading aloud, often due to the reader's inability to decode words

**insertion:** during oral reading, the addition of one or more words that are not in the text

---

A great resource for additional reading terminology is *The Literacy Dictionary* (International Reading Association, 1995).

**instructional-level text:** reading material that is challenging, but not frustrating, to the reader; text that can be read with some instructional support and results in 95 percent or better word recognition and more than 75 percent comprehension

**mispronunciation:** saying words incorrectly during oral reading

> **Example:** A child reads the printed word *like* as *lake* and *present* as *peasant.*

**monotone:** reading in a droning voice without using expression or prosody; no variation in tone, using no inflection so that the reading does not sound like normal spoken language

**multisyllabic words:** words consisting of two or more syllables

**omission:** words from the text that the reader skips or leaves out during oral reading

> **Example:** When reading the sentence *The dogs like to play fetch,* a reader might omit the phrase *like to* and read instead *The dogs play fetch.*

**oral interpretation:** reading text aloud in such a way as to reflect the author's tone, mood, and intent; exhibiting an understanding of what is read

**oral reading fluency:** reading aloud quickly and accurately with expression and understanding

**phrasing:** grouping words into meaningful thought units

> **Example:** An appropriate phrasing of the sentence *The two kids like to play with their friends* is:
>
> *The two kids / like to play / with their friends.*

**prosody:** reading orally using pitch, loudness, tempo, and rhythm to interpret the text with attention to meaning; a fluent reader notices, and gives emphasis to, bold print, capital letters, commas, exclamation marks, and quotation marks; a fluent reader also expressively interprets a text correctly when there are few or no typographical signals

> **Examples:**
> - In the sentence *"Look out!" they shouted, "Here comes a truck!"* the reader would deliver the command with excitement and anxiousness, emphasizing the phrase *Look out.*
> - In the sentence *I am so sorry to hear your sad news,* the reader might drop his or her volume and slow the rate of reading to achieve an apologetic tone.

**punctuation:** typographical signals in the text that guide the reader to pause or interpret the text with expression

**reading rate:** reading text at a certain rate or speed; usually measured by the number of words that are read correctly in one minute (words correct per minute, or wcpm); a child's reading rate may vary depending on the type of text and purpose for reading

**repeated reading:** reading the same text several times, thus increasing word recognition, decoding, phrasing, and expression; an important way struggling readers gain fluency

**repetitions:** repeated words or phrases during oral reading
> Example: When reading the sentence *The boys and girls liked school*, the reader says the word *The* several times before reading the rest of the sentence.

**substitutions:** replacement words for those that appear in a text; often synonyms
> Example: In the sentence *Mary and her mother live in a green house*, the reader uses the word *mom* for *mother* or *home* for *house*.

**text chunking:** breaking a large selection of text into smaller, more manageable sections for instruction

**vocabulary development:** increasing the number of words and word meanings a reader knows

**vocabulary knowledge:** a fund of known words and meanings

**word-by-word reading:** recognizing and orally reading words in a slow, labored manner, characterized by pausing after each word; inappropriate phrasing that inhibits comprehension

**word calling:** reading quickly with rapid word recognition and a lack of appropriate phrasing, punctuation, expression, and prosody; usually accompanied by a lack of comprehension of what is being read

**words correct per minute (wcpm):** measurement taken to assess a child's reading rate; reading a certain number of words correctly per minute

# DISFLUENCY SYMPTOMS CHART

| Symptoms | Component | CHAPTERS 1 AND 2 | | | | | | | CHAPTER 3 | | | | | | | | | CHAPTER 4 | | | |
|---|---|---|---|---|---|---|---|---|---|---|---|---|---|---|---|---|---|---|---|---|---|
| | | Letter-Name Fluency | Letter-Sound Fluency | Sight-Word Fluency | Sight-Word Wall Dictionary | VIP | Multisyllabic Decoding | Text Chunking | Sentence Building | Individual Experience Story | Question Generation | Story Picture Prompts | Sight-Word Books | Subject Paragraphs | Literature Response Stories | Recorded Repeated Reading | Untimed Repeated Reading | Teacher Read-Aloud | Dialogue Theater | Cross-Age Repeated Reading | Interview Strategy |
| Unable to recognize words | Accuracy | X | X | X | X | X | | X | X | X | X | X | X | X | | X | X | X | | X | |
| Unable to decode multi-syllabic words | Automaticity | | X | X | | X | X | X | | | | | | | | | | | | | |
| Reads word by word | Rate | | | | | | | | | X | | X | | | | | | | | X | |
| Reads too slowly | Rate | X | X | X | X | | X | | X | X | | X | | X | X | X | | X | X | | X |
| Reads too fast | Rate | | | | | | | | | | | | | | X | X | | X | X | | X |
| Reads with choppy inappropriate phrasing | Phrasing | | | | | | | | X | X | X | X | X | X | X | X | X | X | X | X | X |
| Ignores punctuation | Phrasing | | | | | | | | | | | | | | X | X | X | X | | | |
| Reads with a lack of expression (monotone) and prosody | Expression and Prosody | | | | | | | | X | X | X | X | X | X | X | X | X | X | X | X | X |
| Lacks appropriate oral interpretation | Expression and Prosody | | | | | | | | | | | | | | | | | | X | | X |
| Doesn't like to practice reading | Motivation | | | | | | | | | | | | | | | | | X | X | X | X |

# CHAPTER 1

# Fluency, the Key to Comprehension

Fluent readers are able to better understand what they read than are their less fluent peers (Kuhn & Stahl, 2000). In fact, current research cited by the National Reading Panel in its 2000 report on teaching reading shows that oral reading fluency is a critical factor in reading comprehension—so critical that the panel named fluency one of the five essential components of effective reading instruction for young children.

# *How Fluency Impacts Comprehension*

**W**hy *is the ability to fluently read aloud so important to a reader's ability to read and understand text?* A look at two very different readers sheds some light on this question.

**Jessi** is a fluent reader. She reads two grades above her grade level and usually has her nose in a book. She reads both narrative and informational text with ease, rarely stumbling over a word. She is often able to sound out unfamiliar words and determine their meaning from the context of the sentence. Jessi reads aloud with such great expression and enjoyment that she brings the voice of the author right off the page. She conveys the appropriate feeling, tone, and mood of the selection. She can put her little brother to bed with a comforting rendition of *Goodnight Moon* or make an audience cheer when she delivers a rousing speech at a Martin Luther King, Jr., Day presentation. When Jessi reads, people listen.

**Justin** is a struggling, disfluent reader who is reading well below his grade level. Justin struggles to sound out phonetically regular words and to recognize basic sight words. He has only one reading speed—slow. When Justin reads aloud, he stumbles over the words and delivers the passage in a labored monotone that wears on him and his listener. Although he wants to be able to read like his more fluent peers, he has so much trouble reading he is embarrassed to pick up a book. When he has a choice of learning activities, he seeks the one that requires the least amount of reading to accomplish.

## ACCURACY AND AUTOMATIC DECODING

Fluent readers like Jessi read quickly with ease and automaticity, recognizing sight words and decoding multisyllabic words by sounding them out or breaking them into recognizable units that they can reconstruct. As they read, fluent readers call on many decoding and word-attack strategies without thinking much about or laboring over the process. In this way, they move along smoothly through the text and complete reading assignments with ease. Because fluent readers expend little effort in decoding, they can rapidly process print and use their cognitive resources to make meaning in these ways:

- to connect words to their meanings (Sinatra, Brown, & Reynolds, 2002; LaBerge & Samuels, 1974)

- to understand the intended meanings of unfamiliar words (Pressley, 2002)

- to keep focused on the meaning of the whole text

Struggling readers like Justin lack automaticity, and this slows them down so that they are unable to complete reading assignments. They often get stuck—and stay stuck—on individual words, unable to recognize or decode them, and therefore, unable to connect the words on the page to their meanings (Pressley & Block, 2002). Because they miss so many words and spend so much energy on each one, they are also unable to process text adequately and to gain meaning from the larger context of the story or passage they read.

### Phrasing, Expression, and Prosody

When fluent readers like Jessi read aloud, they carry expression in their voices and read prosodically, changing their pitch, tone, and rhythm as suggested by the passage. They pay attention to punctuation and typographical signals such as bold print and capital letters to provide emphasis (Opitz & Rasinski, 1998). As fluent readers read, they seek a meaningful delivery by breaking long, multiline sentences into meaningful phrases, even when there are no commas to direct their pauses. These abilities enable them to correctly interpret the text when reading aloud and to better understand what they are reading; they can retell and answer questions about what they have read.

These three girls are using the Dialogue Theater strategy (pages 81–89) to practice reading the dialogue from a favorite story with appropriate phrasing and expression.

Struggling readers like Justin read in a halting, choppy way, moving through a text with word-by-word or choppy two-to-three-word phrasings, while ignoring punctuation and other cues from the text. This keeps disfluent readers from grouping words into meaningful units and impairs their comprehension. They are so busy trying to figure out each word that they can't think about what the author is trying to tell them and how they might give voice to the ideas on the page. Ultimately, this lack of fluency prevents a reader like Justin from understanding, enjoying, and succeeding when reading.

# *Help for Teachers With Struggling Readers*

**W**hat is a teacher with one, several, or a whole class of struggling readers like Justin to do? The first step is to identify specific aspects of fluency that affect these students. Look to the struggling reader portraits in each lesson and read the fluency terms and definitions listed on pages 8–10 to familiarize yourself with the details you're listening for when children read aloud.

The next step is to assess children to gain an understanding of their fluency strengths and weaknesses. Assessing your students' oral reading fluency allows you to hear and identify their difficulties with word recognition, decoding, rate, phrasing, expression, and prosody—all obstacles to fluent reading. Just as oral reading gives you a look at the child's reading process, initial and ongoing fluency assessment enables you to measure a child's progress toward fluency and to assess the effectiveness of your fluency instruction. A more complete discussion of fluency assessment, along with ideas for basic assessment techniques, is provided in Chapter 5.

Finally, you'll need to develop strategies to target those areas in which your struggling readers need help. Refer to the chart on page 11 to find strategy lessons that target specific fluency issues.

In the next section, I begin with lessons that reinforce basic phonics skills that all beginning readers need: the ability to identify the names and sounds that letters produce. Depending on your struggling readers' needs, you may want to skip ahead to later chapters that target strategies for more advanced readers.

# Emergent Reader Strategies

We hope that our first, second, and third graders come to us with all the prerequisite skills and print experiences they need to become great readers. However, we must often back up to the very beginning and tackle the skills our emergent readers need to master before they move on to connected texts at grade level. Letter-Name Fluency and Letter-Sound Fluency are two strategies that you may want to implement with readers at the emergent level.

## Letter-Name Fluency 🔍 🕐

The ability to name letters is one of the fundamental stepping stones in the decoding process. Teachers often introduce emergent readers to letter names by showing children a letter, naming it, and then giving a verbal cue, such as "Circle or point to the *a* on the page." A struggling reader can usually point to the *a* when you have given the letter name as a clue. However, if you point to a letter and ask the child to identify it by name, he or she may be unable to tell you. While stronger readers may be able to identify the letter easily both by name and by appearance, we need to be sure to help struggling readers identify and name written letters quickly and correctly, so they can move on to the next step and properly decode.

### The Problem

The beginning reader has difficulty recognizing and naming letters.

### The Symptoms

Unable to name the letters of the alphabet when presented with the individual letters on flash cards or in sight words

> **Jerome** entered first grade able to name only the letters *d, b, j, r, t, h, u, p, m, e,* and *z*. He often mixed up the letters with numerals. This made it extremely difficult for him to learn and remember letter sounds and beginning sight words, even phonetic ones such as *can* and *go*.

### The Solution

Work with letter naming until the child can quickly and accurately recognize and name each of the 26 letters in random order. Children should be able to identify both upper- and lowercase forms for each letter.

> Every day I worked with **Jerome** and two or three other students who needed similar instruction in a small group. I taught the letters he did not know, while always reviewing the letters he did know. I provided Jerome with specific, direct

instruction; meaningful, active practice; and lots of repeated exposure to the target letters in different contexts. Jerome learned to recognize each letter and to begin connecting the letters to the sounds they made.

### Putting It to Work in Your Classroom

Use Letter-Name Fluency with individuals and small groups of beginning and struggling readers who have similar needs. Begin working with the letters the children see in their names and in the sight words they are learning. Point these letters out to them on the covers and in the pages of books you are reading aloud to them. Learning the letters becomes meaningful for them and easy to remember when they connect the letters to important people and things in their lives.

### I. Preparing and Introducing the Activity

- Secure a small whiteboard and prepare letter flash cards, using two to three letters the children do not know and two to three they already do know.

- Write several words on the board that begin with the target letters (such as a classmate's name or the name of a child's pet). Say the word and point to the new letters. You might explain to children that everyone's name begins with a letter of the alphabet, and they will need to know letters so they can write notes to and read notes from friends and family. This is a great opportunity to point out that names begin with uppercase letters.

- Repeat these procedures, teaching both lower- and uppercase, until children can match the lowercase letters to their uppercase counterparts. Begin by teaching the lowercase letters that the children see in the words in familiar texts and introduce the corresponding uppercase letters as they occur in words you are teaching, such as in the children's names and the names of their classmates, and at the beginning of a sentence.

### 2. Modeling Letter-Name Identification

- Review the names of known letters and introduce new letters one at a time. Show the card as you name the letter. Then write words that contain the letter on the board, and have children find and name the letter in the written words on the board. Repeat with each of the day's target letters.

---

Always review known letters before introducing new ones. Use a checklist to keep track of each of the letters students can identify and those they must still master.

### 3. Guiding Letter-Name Identification

- Use the letter cards you prepared in step 1. You may also use magnetic letters on a magnetic board or on the table in place of the letter cards. The bright colors and shapes may assist children who are visual and tactile learners.

- Ask children to say the letter names as you show them the cards, giving each child a turn. Go through the letter cards several times, challenging the group to name the letters a little more quickly each time.

- Place the letter cards facedown in a pile on the table. Ask each student to turn over a card and name the letter. Name and replace in the stack any missed letter, and call on that same child when the letter appears again. Repeat until each child can name the letters.

- Guide students to write the letters with their fingers in the air as you write them on the board. Describe the letter formation as you write. For example, when writing lowercase *a*, say, "Around, up to meet, and down again makes an *a*." Once students can recognize, name, and write the letters, ask them to write each letter on their papers as you pick up a letter card and say the letter name.

### 4. Extending Letter-Name Learning

*Match It!* Play a matching game with the letter cards. Write each letter on two cards. Lay the cards out facedown. Have students take turns flipping over a letter card, saying the name, and flipping over another card to see if they can find a match. Let them keep score by earning a point for each match they make.

*Letter Bingo* Play Bingo with the letter cards. Write the letters in random order on bingo cards using both lowercase and uppercase letters. Give each child a Bingo card and paper squares to cover the letters. Draw a letter card from your stack and say the name of the letter. Students cover the space on their Bingo boards containing the uppercase and lowercase letter. The winner is the first player to correctly identify and cover five letters in a row on his or her board.

# LETTER-SOUND FLUENCY 🔍 🕐 ✢

**K**nowing the sounds of the letters is crucial to struggling readers' ability to recognize words, and these children need extra support distinguishing among letter sounds. Teach some of the easiest letter sounds first, the ones for which the letter name sounds like the letter sound, such as *b*, *t*, *v*, long *e*, *i*, and *o*, and so on. Note that the letter sounds struggling readers almost always miss are *q*—/*kw*/, *y*—/*y*/, and *w*—/*w*/ because they don't sound like their letter names when they are read. For example, when you say the letter name *y*, your mouth forms a sound more like *wuh*, causing some struggling readers to make the sound for *w* when they encounter a *y* in their reading. In contrast, a much easier letter for a struggling reader is *b*; as the child says the letter name *b*, he or she makes the sound /*b*/. I teach and review letter sounds as I introduce sight words (see Sight-Word Fluency, pages 23–26), because knowing and using the sounds helps children distinguish one word from another.

## The Problem

The beginning reader has difficulty remembering letter sounds.

## The Symptoms

Unable to give the sounds of the consonant letters and short and long vowels when presented with the individual letters on flash cards or in phonetically regular sight words

> **Margo** entered first grade able to say only the sounds for the letters *b, c, m, j, k, p, t, r,* and hard *g*. This made it very difficult for her to learn and remember beginning sight words such as *can, man,* and *go*.

## The Solution

Letter-Sound Fluency enables beginning and struggling readers to recognize phonetically regular sight words. Continue this instruction until each child is able

---

When teaching the sounds of the letters, try to minimize the final *-uh* sound that we attach to most letter sounds. The added *-uh* gets clunky and interferes with blending the letter sounds together to form a word. For example, in sounding out *bit*, pronounce it /*b*/-/*i*/-/*t*/ instead of *buh-i-tuh*. Staying true to the sound of each letter helps children easily blend the sounds of a word together in a way that sounds like the word.

to quickly give the sound of each consonant letter and the short and long vowels when shown the letter in isolation and in the context of short, simple sight words.

> Every day I worked with **Margo** and two to three other students who needed to learn similar letter sounds. Through repeated practice that included seeing the letters in phonetically regular sight words, words from favorite poems, and in classmates' names, Margo learned the sounds of the letters she did not know. She was then able to begin sounding out the words she was learning.

### Putting It to Work in Your Classroom

Use Letter-Sound Fluency with individuals and small groups of beginning and struggling readers who have similar needs. Begin working with the sounds from the phonetically regular sight words they are learning. For instance, if you are teaching the word *man*, teach the sounds for *m*, short *a*, and *n*. Always remember to relate the sounds they are learning to words they are learning.

### I. Preparing and Introducing the Activity

- Secure a small whiteboard and prepare letter flash cards or gather magnetic letters, using two to three letter sounds the children do not know and two to three they do already know.

- Write on the board two phonetically regular sight words that you are teaching that contain the target sounds. You might wish to include a child's name and those of his or her classmates when appropriate. (For example, you might suggest, "Let's list the names of kids in your class whose names begin with *M–mmm*.") Point to the target letters in the words and explain that sounds are like part of a word's fingerprint. Learning to say the sounds for these letters will help children recognize and remember these words.

- Review the known letter sounds and introduce the new sounds one at a time. First say the sound of the letter, and then write the letter on the board while saying the sound. Then have children locate the letter that stands for the sound in the word.

### 2. Modeling Letter-Sound Recognition

- Place the letter cards you created in step 1 in a pile facedown. As you quickly turn the cards over, make the sound of each letter.

### 3. Guiding Letter-Sound Recognition

- Use the letter cards for this activity. You may also want to use magnetic letters in place of letter cards and adapt the procedure accordingly (see the note in step 3 on page 18).

- Ask each child to say the sounds of the target letters as you quickly show him or her the letter cards, challenging the child to go a little more quickly each time. Repeat as necessary.

- Show the child a group of letters containing a target letter and ask him or her to say the sound of the letters as he sorts the cards.

- Place the letter cards in a pile facedown on the table. Ask a child to take a card and say the sound of the letter. If the child misses a letter sound, say the sound for the child and connect it with a familiar word. Then replace the letter in the stack, and call on that child when the letter appears again.

- Say a letter sound and have students write the letter that stands for that sound on their paper.

### 4. Extending Letter-Sound Learning

*Sound Spelling* In this activity, children work from letter sounds to make words. Make sure you have a set of letter cards or magnetic letters for each child. Give children the same four to five letters (including a vowel) for which they know the sounds. Say the initial sound of a three-letter phonetically spelled sight word the children are learning, such as /c/ for *cat*. Have students find the letter that makes that sound and place it in front of them. Repeat with the second letter of the word and then the third letter. Invite students to read the word from the sounds. Students may also write the sounds to make the word.

*Letter-Sound Flip Chart* Make a flip chart with letter cards. Punch a hole in the top of each letter card and put them on a ring. Challenge students to take turns flipping the cards and first saying the sounds of the letters, and then naming a word that has the letter sound. Add new letters as their sounds are taught.

Keep a letter-sound checklist with the letters and corresponding sounds running alphabetically across the top and the children's names listed in the first column. This checklist will help you to remain current on the letter sounds students can identify and those they cannot.

# CHAPTER 2

# Accuracy and Automatic Decoding

**A** struggling reader may have difficulty recognizing sight words and may not be able to sound out unfamiliar words during reading. Missing one in every three words, as some struggling readers do, makes it virtually impossible to read fluently, to understand what words mean, or to gain the meaning of words from context. Imagine a pianist not playing, or leaving out, one in every three notes in a song. It would be impossible to recognize the piece! Readers must be able to quickly recognize or sound out the words if they are to read fluently and gain meaning from text. The strategies in this chapter help children learn to recognize the words they need to know and to decode longer, unfamiliar words, thus freeing them up to process what they read faster and focus on making meaning from the text.

# SIGHT-WORD FLUENCY 🔍 🕐 ✚

Teaching sight words is so important to children's reading success that we need to teach these words with deliberateness and persistence until our students can accurately and automatically identify them. Most of the words children will see in their reading are the basic sight words such as those found on the Dolch Sight-Word List of 220 high-frequency words (excluding nouns) in Appendix A. If children don't recognize sight words, they are absorbing very little information from their reading. These are the words struggling readers need to learn right away.

## The Problem

The beginning reader is unable to quickly recognize sight words.

## The Symptoms

Confuses and is unable to recognize and remember sight words

> **Ralph**, a first grader, had great difficulty learning sight words. He was unable to remember them when shown the words on flash cards. He continually confused words such as *see* and *some*. He often said he couldn't remember the word and just made a guess. This was beyond the scope of context clue work—he missed so many high-frequency words his reading was labored and without comprehension. In addition to strengthening his ability to accurately identify sounds, he needed to be able to recognize and recall a large bank of words immediately.

## The Solution

Use the Sight-Word Fluency strategy in addition to Letter-Sound Fluency activities (pages 19–21) to enable beginning and struggling readers to accurately and quickly recognize basic sight words. The Dolch Sight-Word List gives you an idea of the "bank" of sight words readers should recognize automatically by second grade.

> When I coach primary-grade teachers, we begin teaching sight words in kindergarten and set a goal for students to identify as many of these words as possible by the end of first grade. The first-grade teacher then sends the second-grade teacher an assessment record that highlights the words on the list that a child still does not know. The second-grade teacher does the same for the third-grade teacher. In this way, a child's next teacher immediately begins to review or introduce the words with which they have trouble. You may wish to use this strategy every day throughout the year to help students master as much of the list as they can.

I began by having **Ralph** read the Dolch Sight-Word List to identify the words Ralph did not know. I worked each day with Ralph and several other children to give him lots of opportunities through reading and writing to see and recognize the sight words that he stumbled on in his reading. Since his letter-sound knowledge was also weak, I continued to teach and reinforce letter sounds to enable him to match letter sounds to sight words. By midyear, Ralph had learned to identify almost all of the first 50 sight words.

### Putting It to Work in Your Classroom

Use Sight-Word Fluency with small groups of children who have similar needs. You'll find that you can use the same techniques and strategies to teach sight-word recognition that you rely on to teach letter identification and letter sounds. Begin working with meaningful, high-utility words that children have seen in class texts as well as words necessary for writing and reading simple stories, and, of course, the children's names. (I find books like Dr. Seuss's *One Fish, Two Fish, Red Fish, Blue Fish* great for this work.) These words, taken from the meaningful context of their work and relationships in the classroom, are easy for children to remember. Children often experience success with words that are regularly phonetic. Prioritize these sight words in your lessons.

### I. Preparing and Introducing the Activity

- Prepare sight-word cards or gather magnetic letters (see Appendix A: Dolch Sight-Word List). Select some words the children know and two or three new ones that are very different in shape from one another and that are of high use (for example, *see, can, the, dog*). Show children these target words.

> Choosing words that look different will help students distinguish each word in the group more readily.

- Write on the board or have ready a sentence that has the target words in it.

- Read the sentence aloud smoothly, pointing to each word.

- Ask children to locate the target words in the model sentence. Explain that they will see these words over and over as they read, so they need to learn to recognize them quickly.

- Review the known words on the cards and introduce the new words one at a time, saying the word and discussing the shape of the word. For example, encourage students to notice how two *e*'s look next to one another, as in *see*, or how the letters are tall-short-short-tall in *took*. Ask children to write the words from the board on their paper as you say the word.

## 2. Modeling Sight-Word Identification

- Fluently read aloud the model sentence a second time, and then read the word cards as you show children the target words.

## 3. Guiding Sight-Word Identification

Use magnetic letters, letter tiles, or letters written on cards as well as the sight-word cards you created for this lesson as you complete the following steps.

- Show the first target word and have children name its letters. Put the word aside and give each child the letters he or she needs to spell that word. Ask children to "build" the word, look at the word carefully, and name each letter. Ask them to close their eyes and picture the word, and then check to see if they were correct. Have students mix up the letters, "build" the word again, and then run their finger under the word from left to right while saying the word to check it. Remind them to use the sounds of the beginning and ending letters of the word to help them remember the word. (See the strategies for struggling emergent readers in Chapter 1.)

- Challenge children to say the words quickly as you show them each card in the stack.

- Repeat these steps a few times as appropriate and try one or more of the extension activities below.

- Each day, review known words before introducing new ones. Keep a checklist to remain current on the words each student can identify and those they must still master.

## 4. Extending Sight-Word Learning

You can provide extra practice for children by creating simple sight-word games and activities such as these:

***Sight-Word Match*** Play a matching game with five to ten words from the lesson. Write each word on two cards. Lay the cards out facedown. Have children take turns flipping over a word card, reading it, and flipping over another card to see if they can find a match.

***Sight-Word Bingo*** Play Bingo with sight words when children have learned at least nine sight words. (You will need to fill nine spaces on each three-by-three square board. If you have fewer than nine words, you can write several words twice on a card and have children cover two spaces when that word is called.) For a more challenging game, when children have learned at least 25 sight words, use a five-by-five square board. Write the words in random order on the Bingo boards. Give each child a Bingo board and colorful paper rectangles to cover the words. If you are not playing with a caller, have one child at a time draw a word card from the stack and say the word aloud. All players should cover the space or spaces in which the word appears.

***Sight-Word Mini–Flip Chart*** When you have finished the lesson, create a duplicate set of sight-word cards, punch a hole in the top of each card, and put all the cards on a ring. Show children how to flip the cards and say the words. Then let them do this independently. Challenge them to go a little more quickly each time.

**Check out these two great sight-word resources on the Web:**

- "The Best Thing in the World," a story that includes all of the 220 Dolch words. You can download and print a version at mrsperkins.com/dolch.htm.

- Author Jan Brett's Web site provides illustrated sight-word lists that correspond to her books at janbrett.com/games/jan_brett_dolch_word_list_main.htm.

# SIGHT-WORD WALL DICTIONARY 🔍 ✦

**T**eachers often advise children to use phonetic spelling in their writing to the exclusion of teaching children to correctly spell basic sight words. While encouraging children to spell phonetically facilitates their use of phonics, it usually creates a big stumbling block for struggling readers whose phonics skills are shaky at best. I find it helpful to give struggling readers the tools to correctly spell basic sight words and simple common nouns in their writing; I want these children to practice recognizing and reading the correctly written words from their own writing to increase their word recognition accuracy. This strategy supports readers as they learn to read from their own writing, helping them to become more resourceful spellers.

## The Problem

The beginning reader has difficulty recognizing and spelling sight words.

## The Symptoms

Unable to recognize sight words or to remember how to spell them in independent writing assignments

> **Bonnie**, a first grader, had great difficulty learning to recognize and spell sight words. When she finally recognized the word *go* and then wanted to use it in her writing, she couldn't remember how to spell it. She continually asked for help to spell *go* and other high-utility sight words.

## The Solution

The Sight-Word Wall Dictionary enables beginning and struggling readers to recognize and accurately spell sight words and basic nouns, and other high-utility words. With this strategy, you can add sight words to the wall dictionary throughout the year until all of the 220 Dolch sight words have been taught. You can add other high-utility words children need to use in their writing as well.

> Every day, I gave **Bonnie** opportunities to write and spell sight words and basic nouns in response to writing and reading activities. I reminded her to use the wall dictionary to help her with spelling. Within a short time, she began to look up and use the wall dictionary to locate the correct spelling of sight words. Her spelling and recognition of other sight words improved markedly. She also learned to use the wall dictionary without having to be reminded.

*Putting It to Work in Your Classroom*

Use the Sight-Word Wall Dictionary with classes and small groups of struggling readers with similar needs. You'll want to use this strategy as soon as you begin teaching the sight words. The words you put on the wall dictionary can be meaningful, high-utility words from poems and shared reading that you have been working with in the classroom along with words that are necessary for writing and reading simple stories. Refer children to the wall dictionary to "look up" how to spell these words as they write. Make sure the words are large enough to be read from the farthest seat in the room. Too often I've seen word walls in classrooms with words so small that no one can read them!

## I. Preparing and Introducing the Activity

- Using large print (4" to 6" high) prepare a letter card for each letter of the alphabet and place the cards on the wall around the room from left to right in alphabetical order. These letter cards mark the section of the wall on which the sight-word cards will be placed.

- Using large print again, prepare a word card for each high-utility word as you teach it (see Sight-Word Fluency, pages 23–26).

- Explain to children that they will use these words over and over in their writing and that they will be able to use the wall dictionary to help them until they can spell the words on their own.

- As you build the word wall, include words children collectively continue to misspell in their writing. You may also wish to include the children's names.

## 2. Modeling Fluent Oral Reading

- After teaching a word, read the word aloud and add it to the wall dictionary. Have children use the first letter of the word to guide you in placing the word in the appropriate section.

## 3. Guiding Repeated Oral Reading

Use the wall dictionary for the following activities:

- Call on students each day to read the previously taught words. For example, say,

    "**Susie**, read the words that begin with the same letter that comes at the beginning of your name."

    "**Bill**, can you read our sight words from bottom to top, Z to A?"

    "**Keisha**, what word in the R section means to move or go quickly?"

- When a student asks you how to spell one of the words on the wall, ask, "What letter [or sound] does it begin with? Can you find it?"

## 4. Extending Repeated Oral Reading

***Remember the Words!*** Call out one of the words you and your students have been working with. Have children locate the word on the wall and write it on a sheet of paper. Repeat with other words. For a quick assessment, you can also cover the wall dictionary with butcher paper and ask children to write all the words they can remember from the wall dictionary in five minutes. Then take the cover off and let students see which words they remembered. Collect children's papers and repeat this activity in another month or two so that you and your students can see how their word bank is growing.

# VOCABULARY IDENTIFICATION AND PRACTICE (VIP)

Traditional reading programs tell you to introduce new words prior to reading and to focus primarily on word meaning. Following this approach, struggling readers are usually able to learn (or they may already know) the meanings of these words, but they never learn to decode and recognize them in the lesson text. When you introduce vocabulary, remember that meaning instruction must go hand in hand with word recognition. Use the VIP strategy in conjunction with teaching word meaning. If your vocabulary words include multisyllabic words, use the Multisyllabic Decoding strategy described on pages 33–35.

### The Problem

The struggling reader has difficulty remembering new vocabulary words in text.

### The Symptoms

Unable to quickly and automatically recognize, remember, or decode new vocabulary words in isolation and in text; unable to connect the meanings of words to the corresponding printed words in the text

> **Kevin**, a second grader, loved the science units his teacher presented, but he struggled with the science textbook passages. He had trouble recognizing and decoding new vocabulary words such as *wilderness*, *identical*, *roar*, and *wolves*. In class discussions he could relate the new words to his own experiences and use the words correctly in sentences. However, when he came to these words in the textbook, he could not read them.

### The Solution

Use the VIP strategy to enable beginning and struggling readers to recognize and remember new vocabulary words and to connect the printed words with their meanings. Use this strategy when you introduce new vocabulary words prior to reading a new selection, whether it is a selection in your reading series, a content-area text chapter, or a poem.

> When **Kevin** was given instruction and practice in recognizing new vocabulary words prior to reading, he was able to recognize the words when he came to them in the text. This also enabled him to connect the words to their meanings and to read the text much more fluently.

## *Putting It to Work in Your Classroom*

This strategy helps both classes and small groups of struggling readers who cannot easily remember new vocabulary. Use these ideas to teach children how to recognize new words and connect the words to their meanings.

### 1. Preparing and Introducing the Activity

- Use the words provided in the instructional material or from your own vocabulary list to prepare word cards. In addition, list these words on the board or on a sheet of chart paper.

- Ask children to skim the text for any other words they think they'll have trouble recognizing or decoding. Have them spell the words for you as you add them to the list.

- Teach children to recognize the selected words prior to reading, along with their meanings. Point out unique features of each word on the list so that students can begin to visually and auditorily recognize the words. This might include noting initial letters, word shapes, word sounds, and number of syllables.

- To help children connect the words with their meanings, use mnemonic strategies such as having children find a familiar synonym for each word or come up with a symbol to identify a word.

- If children have difficulty decoding words of three or more syllables, follow the directions for Multisyllabic Decoding.

> Check out these two great resources for developing children's vocabulary and teaching word-study skills: *Bringing Words to Life: Robust Vocabulary Instruction* by Isabel Beck, et al. (Guilford Press, 2002). *The Spelling List and Word Study Resource Book* by Mary Jo Fresch and Aileen Wheaton (Scholastic, 2002).

### 2. Modeling Fluent Oral Reading

- Say each word clearly and then repeat it within the context of a meaningful sentence: *Growl. My two dogs growl when the doorbell rings.*

### 3. Guiding Repeated Oral Reading

- Read each word again, pointing to the word as you say it and having the children say the word after you.

- Have children chorally read the words again as you point to each word. Select the sentences from the book in which the words appear. Write the sentences on the board or chart paper. Have students practice reading the sentences with a partner.

- Let individual children come to the board or chart to read each of the words out loud, pointing to each word as it is read. Repeat until each child accurately and automatically identifies each of the words. If a child mispronounces or has difficulty with a word, pronounce it, and have him or her repeat it. Then have the child finish reading the list, and go back to the word or words he or she missed.

- Review the words each day of your lesson, with the word cards, the sentences containing the vocabulary words from the text, or other activities such as Word ID (below). Be sure children can use the words as well as identify them visually.

### 4. Extending Repeated Oral Reading

*Word ID* Use the word cards you created to play a word identification game. Place the cards in a pile facedown on the table. Have small groups or pairs of students take turns drawing a card and saying the word. If they say the word correctly they score one point. If they can use it in a sentence meaningfully they score two points. If a child misses a word, say the word for him or her and let the child use it in a sentence to earn one point. Then have him or her place the word in the middle of the pile. Let that child try again when the word appears next. (If a different child draws that word card, let the child who missed it jump in. Then have the child who drew the card take another turn.)

# MULTISYLLABIC DECODING ⏰ ✦

**O**lder struggling readers face textbooks and other grade-level reading materials that are full of common, multisyllabic words like *usually*, *disastrous*, and *reducing*—words that are not on the vocabulary list. Struggling readers often know the meanings of these common words but can't get a handle on breaking them down and sounding them out. While the VIP strategy (pages 30–32) is designed to help children learn to recognize and understand the meanings of the vocabulary words, this strategy helps them tackle the multisyllabic words that appear more and more frequently as the grade level of the text increases.

## The Problem

The struggling reader lacks adequate decoding skills.

## The Symptoms

Unable to recognize or decode words of three or more syllables that are in grade-level texts but that are not taught as a part of the vocabulary instruction prior to reading

> **Mark**, a third-grade struggling reader, was unable to decode multisyllabic words such as *imaginary*, *miserable*, and *accidentally* when he came to them in text. He showed no enthusiasm for reading and was an unwilling participant during reading instruction time. He did, however, want very much to read a novel that was well above his instructional level, and chock-full of words of three or more syllables that he had no way to decode.

## The Solution

The Multisyllabic Decoding strategy helps second- and third-grade struggling readers learn to automatically decode words of two or more syllables at a sufficient rate. Continue using this strategy as long as children need support with multisyllabic words.

> Prior to reading the novel, I selected the multisyllabic words that I anticipated would give **Mark** trouble, wrote them in syllables, and provided Mark with plenty of practice decoding them and reading the words in context. Through this process, Mark gained the tools he needed to successfully read the challenging, high-interest novel he chose and was ready to tackle others.

### *Putting It to Work in Your Classroom*

Use Multisyllabic Decoding with struggling readers who are unable to decode words of three or more syllables. You will need to skim the text ahead of time to select words containing three or more syllables that you think the students will have trouble recognizing or decoding. Breaking the words into syllables will help children separate the word into sound and meaning parts they can handle. Text chunking (see page 36) provides more manageable amounts of text to work with, making it easier for children to learn to decode and recognize the words. Taken together, these two strategies will increase readers' ability to decode and recognize these words, to connect the word meanings they already know or have learned to the printed words, and to, therefore, read the text much more fluently.

### I. Preparing and Introducing the Activity

- From the text, select the words of three or more syllables that you think will give your students difficulty when they are reading.

- Explain to children that learning multisyllabic words by syllables will help them learn to decode and recognize many big words. List these words on the board in syllables, grouping the words by their commonalities (for example, all the words that end with a specific suffix, such as *-ly, -ble, -tion, -sion,* or *-ment*; all of the ones that begin with a specific prefix, such as *un-, re-, pro-, non-,* or *bio-*).

- Show children how to break down words with affixes; ask students to determine what the suffix or prefix and the root word mean in each category.

- Ask children to scan the text for challenging words, clap or snap the syllables, and spell for you any multisyllabic words they will have trouble decoding. Add them to the word list.

- Prepare word cards with the words written in syllables.

### 2. Modeling Fluent Oral Reading

- Read aloud each word clearly, pronouncing each syllable as you underscore it with your hand.

### 3. Guiding Repeated Oral Reading

Use the word list on the board and the word cards you created in step 1 for these steps:

- Have children pronounce each word chorally after you read it aloud. Then have them read the list chorally as you point to each word. You may also want to have them use the word cards to practice with a partner. Have them read aloud the word and tell what it (or each syllable) means and use it in a sentence.

- As students gain familiarity with this word list, encourage them to search for more words that fit the categories listed in step 1. Help them learn to sound out the words by breaking the words into affixes and roots if they can. Also teach them to think of other words they know that have the same base to seek meaning (for example, if children know *furious* means very angry, then you can help them find the meaning of the noun form *fury*, or extreme anger).

- Provide ongoing instruction in small groups again during the day to children who have difficulty with multisyllabic words. Use sentences that highlight the meanings of the words and the decoding activity included below.

## 4. Extending Repeated Oral Reading

***Self-Competition Decoding*** Use the list of target words with an individual child or a small group of children. Challenge each child to compete with him- or herself. Ask for a volunteer to read the words. Write the child's name on the board. Place a tally next to the student's name each time he or she reads a word correctly. Congratulate the child, read aloud the words he or she missed, and have the student read the list again. Add a tally mark each time the child correctly reads one of the words he or she previously missed. Have children try to read more of the words with each repeated turn, so that eventually they read all of them. When the activity is over, ask the children how they will remember the words that were the most challenging to recall. See if you can help them make a visual or other mnemonic link.

In small groups, readers experiencing the most difficulty usually volunteer to read last, which gives them time to hear the words read repeatedly by the others.

# Text Chunking 🔍 ✦ 🎭

## Why not give struggling readers only instructional-level texts to read?

In addition to supporting struggling readers with texts they can more easily manage, we need to help struggling readers tackle grade-level text. We sometimes challenge our struggling readers with grade-level reading materials because we need to prepare all of our students to take state and standardized tests, which are written on grade level, and often because our schools expect us to use the grade-level textbooks provided in class to teach all students the same grade-level content.

Text chunking is a way to break lengthy text into manageable sections, enabling struggling readers to handle difficult text. It also gives them time to practice the repeated reading of the text to develop appropriate phrasing, expression, and prosody, and to improve their rate. This technique supports the strategy lessons in this chapter. Used in conjunction with VIP (pages 30–32) and the Multisyllabic Decoding (pages 33–35), text chunking gives your struggling readers the time they need to learn to recognize and decode words and to learn their meanings.

### TEXT CHUNKING TIPS

- Chunk the selection you are working on in class into short, manageable sections. For instance, if the story in your reading basal is seven pages long, divide it into sections of two to three pages. If you are reading a long chapter or section in a social studies or science textbook, use the chapter subheadings to guide you. If the content and vocabulary are very challenging, select only one section at a time.

- When you have selected the section to present to your struggling readers, be sure to teach the vocabulary and build background for the content prior to having children read the section.

- Vary the way students read aloud the section. For example, you might have students read alternating pages or paragraphs with a partner or place children in small groups of three to four, assign a part of the section to each group to practice reading chorally, and then call on the groups in order to read their parts so that the group can read and hear the whole selection fluently.

- If your struggling readers can't finish the whole chapter or assigned section and the rest of the class needs to move on, select the most important sections for these students to practice and read the rest to them, or let them listen to a recorded reading of the section.

# CHAPTER 3

# Accuracy, Phrasing, and Expression

**A** struggling reader may have difficulty not only recognizing words but also stringing words together in phrases and sentences. This can make understanding the meaning of the words on a page even more difficult. Reading a story word-by-word or with awkward phrasing is like reading sheet music by playing each note without looking at the notes and holds in the surrounding bar; the notes only sound right together when they are played by a musician in sequence and grouped properly. Readers have to work like musicians, looking ahead of and around each word to understand and deliver it as part of the surrounding phrase, sentence, and paragraph. The lessons in this chapter help you give children the tools they need to continue building accuracy in decoding, break text into meaningful units so that their phrasing enhances their comprehension, and read aloud with appropriate expression.

# Sight-Word Sentence Building 🔍 ✣ 🎼

**S**truggling readers often need help making the transition from recognizing sight words in isolation on flash cards to recognizing and reading those same words in the context of sentences—they often cannot make that connection without support. Sight-Word Sentence Building is one in a progression of strategies: reading isolated words (see Sight-Word Fluency, pages 23–26), reading the words in a sentence, and finally, reading the words in a simple text of several sentences on a page (see Sight-Word Books, pages 61–64).

### The Problem

The beginning reader has difficulty reading basic sight words in text.

### The Symptoms

Unable to recognize and read basic sight words in simple sentences

> **William,** a first grader, had trouble remembering his basic sight words and difficulty with one-to-one correspondence when he read words in text. Sometimes, when he was able to recognize the sight words on flash cards, he was unable to recognize and read those same words in sentences. This was extremely frustrating to him. His poor sight-word recognition caused him to read very slowly and to doubt his own reading ability.

### The Solution

Sight-Word Sentence Building enables beginning and struggling readers to read simple sight-word text with the appropriate accuracy, phrasing, and expression. Use the Dolch Sight-Word List (Appendix A) and the Basic Noun List (Appendix B) to guide your choice of words for building sentences, or use the reproducible sight-word cards on pages 42–43 with the suggested sentences on page 44 for a ready-to-use lesson.

> I worked with **William** every day along with two to three other children. He liked building a sentence, putting the punctuation card at the end, and then practicing reading the sentence aloud. He liked pointing to the words as he read and he especially liked mixing up the word cards for his peers. This gave him the practice he needed to make the transition from recognizing individual sight words to recognizing the words in the context of a sentence. William began to recognize more and more of the words both in isolation and in sentences. His reading of the sentences became more accurate and automatic and his ability to phrase correctly improved. William eventually was able to build and fluently read his own simple one- and two-line sight-word sentences.

### Putting It to Work in Your Classroom

Use the Sight-Word Sentence Building strategy with small groups of children who need help making the transition from recognizing words in isolation to reading them in sentences. Begin with three to four meaningful, phonetically regular, high-utility words that you are already working with in the classroom. This will enable children to use the letter sounds they are learning to help them remember the new words.

To create a set of word cards for sentence building, select a group of words such as *can*, *go*, and *I*, that together will form a sentence. Include in the set nouns such as *man*, *boys*, and *girls* (see the Basic Noun List) as well as children's names—children love to use classmates' names to build sentences! Also include words such as *The*, *Boys*, *Girls*, *Can*, with the first letter capitalized so that these can be used at the beginning of a sentence, and cards with end marks such as a period and a question mark. (You may find when you first begin using the period card, beginning readers will say the word *period* when they come to that card. This is a fine way for them to note that they have come to the end of a sentence and to reinforce their print-awareness skills.) Continue with the sentence building until the children are able to fluently read the simple one- and two-line sight-word sentences.

### I. Preparing and Introducing the Activity

- Prepare the word cards as described above. Review the known words in the card set and introduce the new words one at a time, saying the word and discussing its shape. Have children find the new word in a familiar text, such as a class rules list or a book they are reading. Write the word on the board while saying the word.

- On a small whiteboard, write the target sentence and read it fluently to the children.

- Explain that they will learn to "build" and read this sentence fluently.

- Arrange children at a table so that they are sitting across from you. Build the sentence so that the cards face right side up for the children.

| I | can | go | . |
|---|-----|-----|---|

## 2. Modeling Fluent Oral Reading

- Each time you build and introduce a new sentence, put the word cards in order and read the sentence through, pointing to each word as you read it.

## 3. Guiding Repeated Oral Reading

You may want to use the reproducible word and punctuation cards provided on pages 42–43 and the suggested one- and two-line sentences on page 44 to complete the following activities.

- Ask each child to read the sentence and point to each word as he or she reads it. Let children try it a second time in order to read it smoothly.

- Mix up the cards. Have the group work together with your help to sort the cards, build the sentence, and read it smoothly.

- Mix up the cards and give them to one student at a time. Ask the child to build the sentence and read it smoothly, grouping the words in a way that sounds like he or she would say it. You may need to read aloud the sentence for the child again to help him or her find the right order. Repeat the sentence until he or she can build it correctly and read it fluently with appropriate phrasing and expression.

- Have the child mix up the cards and hand them to the next child. Repeat until each child has had a turn.

- See if children can suggest an alternate way to arrange the cards. Or you might change one card to make a new sentence with a different meaning. Let them practice reading the new sentence fluently.

| Can | I | go | ? |

## Building and Reading Two-Line Sentences

When children are able to build and fluently read one-line sentences, demonstrate how to build longer sentences that break at the end of, and continue underneath, the first line. Show students how to fluently read a two-line sentence by running your finger under the words as you read, emphasizing directionality (at the end of the first line they will see you drop down to the second line and begin tracking the words from left to right again). Have them share examples from a favorite book.

| The | boys | and | girls | can |
|---|---|---|---|---|

| run | and | jump | up | . |
|---|---|---|---|---|

## 4. Extending Repeated Oral Reading

Use the word and punctuation cards you prepared in step 1 with these activities.

***Sentence-Building Zone*** Challenge children to create their own sentences. Mix up five or six word cards and a set of punctuation cards and spread them out faceup on the table. (Include only words that children know.) Invite each child to build and fluently read his or her own sentence.

***Build-and-Read Sentence Center*** In a quiet work area, place sets of sentence word cards and sample sentences in envelopes, resealable plastic bags, or other containers, and set out writing paper and pencils. Have children build a sentence, write it on a sheet of paper, and read it to a classmate. Students may also keep a set of the word cards at their desks in a plastic bag or envelope to practice building, writing, and reading their sentences. You may also have them take a set home to use with family members.

# Sight-Word Cards

| | |
|---|---|
| see | and |
| jump | Dad |
| dog | Mom |
| cat | I |
| up | boys |
| down | girls |

# Sight-Word Cards (continued)

| | |
|:---:|:---:|
| **can** | **a** |
| **go** | **Can** |
| **run** | **The** |
| **man** | **.** |
| **the** | **?** |

# Sight-Word Sentences to Build

## One-Line Sentences

I can go.

The man can go.

I see the man.

I can see the man.

I can see the man go.

Can I see the man?

Can I jump?

The man can jump.

Can the man jump?

I can jump up.

Can the cat jump up and down?

I see a man.

Can I see the man go?

The man can jump up.

I can run.

I can jump down.

The man can run.

The man can jump down.

The dog can run.

I see the dog.

The dog can see.

The man can see the dog.

## Two-Line Sentences

Can the cat and dog jump up
and down?

The man and I can run
and jump up.

I can see the man jump up
and down.

The cat and the dog can jump
up and down.

The boys and girls can run
and jump up and down.

Mom and Dad can see the cat
and the dog.

Dad can see the cat and the dog
jump up and down.

Can Mom and Dad see the cat
and the dog?

# INDIVIDUAL EXPERIENCE STORY

Children enter school in the fall full of expectation. Children who haven't yet learned to read or who cannot read well expect to become readers and writers—and we want to do everything in our power to invite them into the literate community. I always have my first-grade nonreaders begin to read on the first day of school. I do this by teaching them to read from their own dictated story sentence. By reading their own words they can recall and repeat their story, using appropriate phrasing and expression. This strategy is a confidence booster and a great reference point for word building; you will find that even two to three weeks after children have dictated their stories they can still read what they have written. Having struggling readers frequently revisit sentences they have constructed reinforces word recognition and supports fluent reading.

## The Problem

The struggling reader has difficulty recognizing words and fluently reading simple text.

## The Symptoms

Unable to recognize sight words in simple text and reads word-by-word, demonstrating choppy phrasing and a lack of expression

**Courtney** was a small, wiry child with a sparkle in his eye and a penchant for getting into mischief. He entered first grade with little prior experience with print and qualified for a special reading assistance class. He had trouble learning sight words and stumbled through simple text. Although Courtney was behind the other first graders academically, he was a smart child and he loved the computer.

## The Solution

Writing an Individual Experience Story with beginning and struggling readers enables them to fluently recognize and read sight words and nouns from texts they have created. Continue until children are able to write their own experience stories and read them aloud accurately with appropriate phrasing and expression.

On the very first day of school, **Courtney** dictated a two-sentence story and I printed it on the board in phrases. With my help he read his story several times until he could read it fluently to the class. I printed his story on a piece of paper and taped it to the computer. Courtney typed his story and printed two copies. We put one copy on the wall for display and he took the other home to read to his family. Courtney loved typing, printing, and reading his stories aloud. As the year progressed, he also helped his classmates tell and publish their stories. Through this process, Courtney became a fluent, motivated, and confident reader.

## Putting It to Work in Your Classroom

Use the Individual Experience Story strategy with classes or small groups of children who have similar needs. You can begin using this strategy on the very first day of school by having the children dictate stories about common experiences, such as what games they played last year during recess, or personal experiences, such as what they plan to do after school.

Call on a different child each day to dictate a story. (I find that using the class roll is the easiest way for me to keep track of whose turn it is, and it also lets the children joyfully anticipate their turn.) Write each story on a sheet of chart paper taped to the board so that children can come to the board, read, and point to their words. Keep the stories and revisit them several days later, encouraging children to expand their sentences with descriptive words. You'll find that increasing the complexity and length of their stories builds children's oral reading fluency.

> One first-grade teacher who used this strategy found her children in competition with one another to see who could "write" the longest story! She had wondered why her students' experience stories were getting longer and longer each day, and discovered that the children were going home and writing their stories ahead of time with help from their families so theirs would be longer than the story of the child who had shared before them. Talk about motivation for reading! Not only were they dictating longer stories, they were able to read them as well.

## I. Preparing and Introducing the Activity

- Select a child to dictate a story.

- Have him or her select a story topic (see the list of sample story topics on page 50) and discuss the topic with the group or class to help the child generate the main idea. If you are working one-on-one with a child, you may prompt him or her with questions such as "What are you going to do this afternoon when you get home? What is your story going to be about? What is a good name for the story you are going to write?" Agree on a title (see page 50 for suggestions) and print it at the top of a sheet of chart paper.

- Ask, "Who will be the author of the story?" or "Whose story is it?" and print the child's name under the title (e.g., "by Courtney"). You may want to vary the procedure by asking children to dictate their stories first and then give you a title when they've finished.

- Ask the child to dictate his or her story. Write the dictation on the chart paper, indenting the first line and supporting phrasing by keeping words that belong together on the same line and separating the phrases of a sentence with extra spaces (see the example below). Be sure to write the sentences children dictate with accurate punctuation and spelling so that they learn to recognize words and ideas written correctly from their "writing." When you finish writing, point out print cues in the text, such as indenting the first line, which support appropriate phrasing.

In this dictated story, I left spaces between phrases to encourage Courtney to correctly group the words when he reread his story.

### 2. Modeling Fluent Oral Reading

- Read the child's story fluently, pointing to the words while reading the text, emphasizing appropriate phrasing so that children know to take their time and string words together that fit together.

### 3. Guiding Repeated Oral Reading

- Have the child come to the board and read his or her story aloud. Encourage the child to repeat the story once or twice to read it fluently. (A pointer is helpful and children love using one!) Read in unison with the child as needed.

- Ask for volunteers to read the story aloud or have the whole class or group read it chorally. You may find that all of the children want a turn!

- Print the child's story on paper and put it at the computer where he or she can see it. Have the child type the story, print two copies, and practice reading it aloud to a classmate or to the class. Post one copy in the classroom, and let the child take the other home to read to a family member. More able readers can act as editors and assist classmates with the writing and reading of their stories. Have the editor add his or her name at the bottom of the page (e.g., "Editor: Samuel").

Before sending children off to type their stories on the computer, be sure to point out how to center a title, indent the first sentence, capitalize the first letter of the first word in each sentence, and end each sentence with a period, question mark, or exclamation point.

- Make a book of each child's stories, place the books together in your class library, and have children practice orally reading their own and others' books during independent or partner reading time.

- As children become more proficient at reading their stories, substitute the child's name (and *he* or *she* where appropriate) for the word *I*, and change the corresponding pronouns, setting the story in third-person narrative. This makes it easier for children to read one another's stories. You may want to make a lesson of this by working from several of the children's story sentences

Courtney's story told in third person with appropriate pronoun substitutions.

on the board. For each sentence, erase each pronoun and draw a horizontal line above it. Ask the children to tell you the pronoun that would fit on the line and write it in for them. Then have the author and volunteers again read the story aloud. Discuss with children how the story stayed the same but who tells it changed.

● For an added challenge, have children tell their story using a different time frame. For example, a story set in past tense beginning *Yesterday I washed my dog . . .* could be set in the future (*Tomorrow I will wash my dog . . .*). Have children read aloud and compare the two stories and notice that the action words change when the time changes.

● When children are able to dictate and fluently read aloud their experience stories, have them write an experience story on their own. (See the sample student story below).

Vernon chose the topic "What I did this morning before school" and gave the story his own title.

| Sample Story Topics and Titles | |
|---|---|
| What I did yesterday after school | *After School, Yesterday After School* |
| What I did this morning before school | *This Morning, Before School* |
| What I like to do on the weekends | *My Weekend, My Trip to the Mall* |
| What my friend and I like to do | *My Friend and I, _____ and I* |
| What I like to do on Saturdays | *My Saturday* |
| What I will do this afternoon | *This Afternoon* |
| What I will do today after school | *Today After School* |
| How I got to school this morning | *My Bus Ride to School* |

## 4. Extending Repeated Oral Reading

***Class or Group Experience Story*** Let each child contribute a sentence to a story. The story may be about a class trip, a school or class visitor, a person the children have interviewed (see The Interview Strategy, pages 92–94), a story they've read, or a content area topic you're studying in class. As each student dictates his or her sentence, write it on the board. Read the completed story aloud fluently for the group and then call on individuals to read it. Type the story and give a copy to them to practice reading with partners. You'll want to repeat this activity on a weekly or biweekly basis. When the group has written four or five experience stories, have children compile the stories in a book to read in class and take home to read to family members.

# Experience Story Question Generation 🔍 🎼

Struggling readers, particularly the first graders I work with, frequently don't phrase their thoughts as questions. Instead they make statements, or commands. They also have difficulty recognizing and reading question-starting verbs (*may, can, will, could, would, should*), adverbs (*why, how*), and pronouns (*who, what*). The question-generation strategy gives struggling readers practice phrasing their own questions. Through reading and writing meaningful questions, they learn to recognize and recall question-starting words and to phrase interrogative sentences accurately in their oral reading.

## The Problem

The struggling reader has difficulty recognizing question words and reading questions.

## The Symptoms

Unable to recognize common words that introduce questions (*who, what, where, when, why, how*) and to read questions and response choices with appropriate intonation, phrasing, and expression

**Melanie** entered first grade lacking the language skills she needed to learn to read successfully. One area she found particularly challenging was using interrogative sentences in her speech and reading them in simple texts. When she wanted to ask for something, she usually made a statement in place of a question, such as "I want a pencil," instead of "May I have a pencil?" She also had trouble learning to recognize words that introduced questions and would mix them up, reading the word *who* for the word *what*, and the word *when* for *where*. She was, however, eager to learn to read and loved being read to.

## The Solution

This strategy builds on the previous strategy lesson, Individual Experience Story. Answering and then asking questions about their own personal experience story helps beginning and struggling readers increase their recognition of question words and fluently read questions and response choices.

**Melanie** developed fluency as she learned to read her own experience stories and to generate questions from them. She learned to ask who, what, where, when, which, why, and how questions from her own stories and those of her classmates. She was also better able to answer questions her peers asked about their stories. Once Melanie could orally ask and answer her own and others' questions, I began writing her questions on the board and providing response choices. Melanie soon learned to fluently read the questions and item choices I wrote from her experience stories and those of her classmates, and to select the correct answers to the questions.

### Putting It to Work in Your Classroom

Use the Experience Story Question Generation strategy with classes and small groups of children who have similar needs. Begin by guiding a student to dictate a one- to three-sentence story about a personal experience (see pages 46–49). You'll find you can begin generating oral questions from a child's individual experience story once all of the children are able to fluently read the child's story. Be sure to include the question words on the Wall Dictionary (see the strategy lesson on pages 27–29) as you teach them.

### I. Preparing and Introducing the Activity

- Prepare word cards with the question words *who, what, where, when, how,* and *why.*

- Select an experience story that children are familiar with and that all of them can fluently read. Post the chart paper on the board.

- Ask the author a question about his or her story. Model a "Who?" question, asking, "Who is this story about?" and have the child answer in a complete sentence ("This story is about me."). Then ask the child to ask a peer the same question.

> When you model a question, young children may actually have to practice repeating the question after you. (I remember saying to one first grader at the beginning of the year, "I want you to ask, 'Who is this story about?'" She then repeated verbatim, "I want you to ask, 'Who is this story about?'")

- When a child answers, ask the questioner, "Is that correct? Did he or she give you a complete sentence? Do you accept the answer?" If needed, say the answer in a complete sentence for the child who is answering and have him or her repeat it after you.

- Repeat with each question word. You may want to see if students can come up with a different question about the story than the one you pose ("Who is Courtney's friend?").

- Write each question below the story on the chart paper. You may want to include the answer in a different color after each question. Encourage children to read aloud the question and answers with proper intonation.

## Generating Oral Questions

### Yesterday After School
### by Courtney

Yesterday after school   Courtney rode
his bike. He went over   to his friend
Robbie's house. They had   chocolate cookies
and milk   for a snack.

**Who** is this story mostly about?
*It is mostly about Courtney.*

**Where** did Courtney go?
*He went over to his friend Robbie's house.*

**What** did they have for a snack?
*They had chocolate cookies and milk.*

**When** did Courtney go to Robbie's house?
*He went yesterday after school.*

**How** did Courtney get to Robbie's house?
*He rode his bike.*

**Why** did he go to Robbie's house?
*He went to Robbie's house because he likes to play with Robbie/ because Robbie is his friend.*

- When all of the children can orally ask and answer *who, what, where, when, why,* and *how* questions from their own stories and the stories of others, write one of their questions with two response choices on the board.

## Generating Written Questions

Jeff and his brother played outside. They played with their dog Baxter.

1. What did Jeff and his brother do?
   - They played with friends.
   - They played with their dog.

2. Where did the boys play?
   - They played in the house.
   - They played outside.

- Once students can read and answer one question per story, write more than one question per story.

### 2. Modeling Fluent Oral Reading

- Review with children the question words on the cards you created in step 1.

- Read aloud the questions and response choices you just recorded. Emphasize proper intonation for interrogative sentences.

### 3. Guiding Repeated Oral Reading

- Use several experience stories with two written questions and several answer choices. These can be typed or photocopied or posted on chart paper.

- Either monitor student work in pairs or work with individual children.

- Have one partner read the question and two answer choices and have the other read the correct answer choice.

- Then ask partners to choose a new story and switch roles.

I find that Experience Story Question Generation helps children not only remember question words and read them fluently in text, it also gives them practice reading the question words in a context similar to the one they will encounter on tests.

## 4. Extending Repeated Oral Reading

Use the question word cards and student stories to complete this activity.

***Just Ask Me*** Write one of the student's experience stories on the board or on chart paper and give each student one of the question cards. Students take turns asking a question from the story that begins with the word on the card they have been given. Students call on others to answer their question. The group must agree that the answer is correct before another child takes a turn. Have children swap cards and time themselves to ask and answer all the questions in under three minutes.

***Question the Class*** After your next read-aloud, let children choose two question words and then write two questions about the story. Invite children to read one of their questions to the class after a second read-aloud. This will support their reading practice as well as help the class build comprehension skills.

## STORY PICTURE PROMPTS 🔍 🎼 ✷

**C**hildren rarely get enough daily practice writing stories and compositions, nor do they have adequate opportunity to read their writing. Yet, guiding students to write and reread their writing is one way for them to become more fluent readers. I find that offering different types of writing prompts is a motivating way to improve my struggling readers' writing and reading. A picture prompt of a familiar animal or object gives them a visual image for reference, making it easier to generate words to include in their writing. This strategy also encourages them to work with the sight words they are learning, including simple nouns, such as common animals and objects. These useful words become a solid part of their spelling and reading repertoire as they write and reread their writing.

### The Problem

The struggling reader has difficulty recognizing and reading basic words in simple text.

### The Symptoms

Unable to remember basic words or to read them in simple text; reads simple text slowly with inappropriate phrasing and expression

> **Sally,** a first grader, had great difficulty recognizing the sight words in simple text. She stopped frequently during reading to try to remember words. These hesitations cause her to read very slowly with a mixture of word-by-word and choppy phrasing.

### The Solution

The Story Picture Prompts strategy enables beginning and struggling readers to fluently read basic words in the context of their own writing, using appropriate phrasing and expression. The picture prompt is a scaffold that also helps children jump-start their writing. Once they have experienced success in communicating several stories with prompts, they often become motivated to write stories without prompts. As their writing improves, so does their reading.

> **Sally** loved coloring pictures and using the sight words she was learning to describe the pictures and tell stories about them. She loved reading aloud her own sentences and stories to others. She did a great job coloring a picture of her dog (black with brown spots) and describing how he looked and what he liked to do. With this practice, Sally learned to connect familiar words to pictures and read her own stories in a fluid, narrative voice. Soon she was able to transfer her phrasing skills to smoothly read short sentences in simple picture books.

### Putting It to Work in Your Classroom

Use Story Picture Prompts with a class or a small group of children who have similar needs. I find that using the animals, objects, and creatures pictured in the literature I read aloud to children is a great way to motivate them to respond in writing and then to read what they have written. For instance, I have discovered that after reading P. D. Eastman's *Big Dog, Little Dog* to my students, they enjoy coloring and writing about the dog, which I present as a picture prompt.

Beginning and struggling readers and writers find it easier to write when prompted by pictures of familiar things, and they enjoy sharing their stories with the class. This also provides them with the frequent repetition of familiar words and opportunities to increase their use of appropriate phrasing and expression. Once children are able to write a simple response to the picture prompt on their paper, you can have them respond on lined paper to a class picture prompt, giving them a list of words they may use in their responses (see below). Eventually you may lead them to respond to a piece of literature they have listened to or read (see the sample student story on page 58).

### 1. Preparing and Introducing the Activity

- Make a copy of the Picture Prompt Sheet (page 60) and draw a familiar picture at the top of the page or use a resource such as clip art to paste in a picture. Write the title above the picture (for example, *The Motorcycle* or *The Duck*). See the Picture Prompt Ideas on page 59.

- Distribute a copy of the prompt sheet to each child. Show the picture and discuss it. Ask children to tell you the words they will need for the title and their story when they write, and list the words on the board or a sheet of chart paper. Use words from the student sample (for example, for *The Duck—water, wild, fly, swim, green, head, quack*).

- Pronounce the words as you point to them.

- Ask children to read the words. You may need to review some of the words several times.

Picture prompts with favorite animals get children excited about telling a story. I record the words they want to use for their stories below the picture. Children return to both the picture and the word bank as they write.

● Ask children to color and write about the picture on their own page.

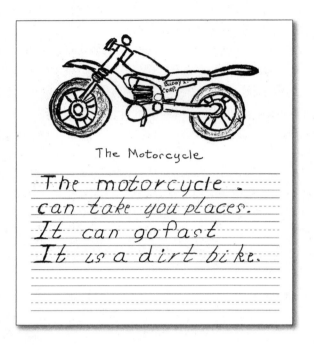

The Motorcycle

The motorcycle can take you places. It can go fast It is a dirt bike.

My struggling readers really love cars, trucks, and motorcycles. I photocopied this motorcycle drawing by an older student onto a picture prompt sheet and it became a high-interest writing prompt. I let children talk and then write about it. The finished descriptions became reading material that the children were able to return to again and again to read and enjoy.

## 2. Modeling Fluent Oral Reading

● Write one child's story on the board or on chart paper. Read the child's story fluently.

## 3. Guiding Repeated Oral Reading

● Have the group read the story chorally, following your phrasing and intonation.

● Let children practice reading their own story to a partner while you monitor the group. Have them read it through several times until their partner agrees that the reading is smooth.

## 4. Extending Repeated Oral Reading

***Hi-Tech Stories*** Have children work with a simple graphics program like KidPix® to pick a piece of clip art or draw their own picture on-screen. Then have them write a story about the picture below the image. Let them print their stories, practice reading them with a partner, and then read them to the class.

## Picture Prompt Ideas

**Animals** cat, dog, cow, fox, kitten, puppy, calf, squirrel, pig, horse, pony, turtle, hen, duck, bat, kangaroo, bear, rabbit, chicks, tortoise, duck, deer, lion, tiger, elephant, camel

**Vehicles** bike, bus, SUV, pickup truck, semi, motorcycle, wagon, train, race car, tow truck, school bus, bicycle, fire engine

**Amphibians, insects, and other creatures** Teddy bear, frog, caterpillar, ladybug, butterfly, beetle, earthworm, ant, snake

Name _____ Date_____

# Picture Prompt Sheet

# SIGHT-WORD BOOKS

**T**eachers often have to teach sight words without a student text that uses these words in context. As my struggling readers learn sight words, I provide them with sight-word-rich sentences in a picture-book format. This strategy gives them multiple opportunities to encounter the words they are learning in a simple text of several sentences on a page. Reading the story increases their ability to read this text fluently and boosts their confidence. Struggling readers also enjoy coloring the pictures, which gives them ownership of the books—and assures that they go back and reread them.

## The Problem

The beginning reader has trouble reading text containing sight words.

## The Symptoms

Doesn't recognize sight words and basic nouns in simple text; reads word-by-word; is unable to read simple text with appropriate phrasing and expression

> **Demetrius**, a first grader, was overwhelmed by much of the grade-level reading material available in the classroom. He read word-by-word and often confused words when he was reading, stumbling over sight words and basic nouns. He wanted so much to remember the words to stories. He needed lots of practice making the transition from recognizing the words in isolation to reading them in text.

## The Solution

The Sight-Word Books strategy assists beginning and struggling readers to quickly and accurately read sight words and basic nouns in simple teacher-created texts. The Dolch Sight-Word List (Appendix A) and the Basic Noun List (Appendix B) can be used to guide your selection of the high-utility words to use in the sight-word books you create. Since you control the complexity of the sentences and the length of the story, these books can be leveled precisely for your struggling readers. Use these books with your students until they are able to fluently make the transition from isolated words to the words in simple text.

> **Demetrius** had many opportunities to practice reading the sight-word books I created for him and his classmates. He enjoyed working on a new page each day and putting his book together. He also liked having a book he could easily read, and he read each book many times. Through this practice, Demetrius learned to fluently read simple grade-level texts containing basic sight words and basic nouns.

### *Putting It to Work in Your Classroom*

Use Sight-Word Books with classes and small groups of struggling readers who have similar needs. Create the simple text for the books using the meaningful, high-utility words you are working on in the classroom. For children gaining proficiency in letter-sound identification, using regularly phonetic words allows the children to sound out words as they read.

### I. Preparing and Introducing the Activity

- Select a topic for the book and use previously taught sight words. (I find that it is best to write the sight-word books around topics that are age appropriate for and of interest to the children, such as animals.)

- To prepare the pages of the sight-word book, hand-print or use a large point size in a word processing program. Each book page should contain only one or two sentences with space above for a simple drawing that you or the children can make. On the final page of the book, present the entire story in a single passage. This will give children practice reading the paragraph format (see the sample story on page 64).

- Introduce one page of the story each day.

- Review target sight words and read the text on the page aloud fluently for children.

- Have students read the page and color the illustration or draw their own.

- When each page has been completed and read, compile each child's pages into a book and have them design the cover.

### 2. Modeling Fluent Oral Reading

- Read the full text on the last page fluently, emphasizing phrasing, with the children following along.

### 3. Guiding Repeated Oral Reading

- Monitor children as they reread with a partner any page they have struggled with. You may need to ask a child to read the page several times, guiding their fluency.

- Check that each child can read the last page smoothly, with accurate phrasing.

- Let students who are able to fluently read the book write their own book on the topic and share it with a classmate (see Create-a-Book Center, next page).

### 4. Extending Repeated Oral Reading

***Create-a-Book Center*** Provide a book-making area where children can author their own sight-word books. Include a list of the sight words they have learned and remind students to use the Sight-Word Wall Dictionary (see pages 27–29) to help them spell familiar words. Stock the center with pencils, crayons, blank paper, and copies of the Picture Prompt Sheet (page 60). You may want to scaffold their writing by supplying pictures related to the current sight-word book. They can paste the picture at the top of a Picture Prompt Sheet and write about it at the bottom. When students have created their own books, have them practice reading the books to one another and then to the class.

# Make-Your-Own Sight-Word Book

I created this simple book in a few minutes using a word processing program, typing the text at the bottom of each of five pages. I used sight words the children were learning, including *fish, blue, run, like,* and *see* to write the sentences. Then I made a printout of the pages and drew a few simple outlines of a fish that children could color according to the story description. To prepare the lesson for a group I made photocopies and stapled the pages into booklets. You may wish to leave the top of each page blank and have children make their own drawings, which may save time and help you gauge their comprehension.

A Fish

by _____

1

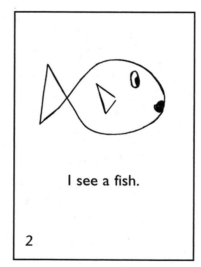

I see a fish.

2

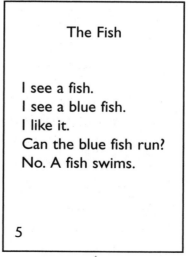

I see a blue fish.
I like it.

3

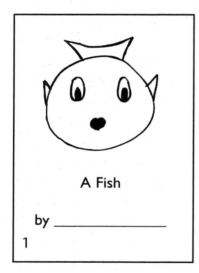

Can the blue fish run?
No. A fish swims.

4

The Fish

I see a fish.
I see a blue fish.
I like it.
Can the blue fish run?
No. A fish swims.

5

# SUBJECT PARAGRAPHS

Like the Individual Experience Story (pages 45–50), Subject Paragraphs gives struggling readers the practice they need writing and reading meaningful text—text that contains the words that are important to their own lives and experiences. The goal is for students to generate text using words that name and describe familiar places, like school and home, and objects and people found in those places. The greater the child's attachment is to the words he or she is reading, the more quickly the child retains those words and the stronger his or her desire is to read.

## The Problem

The beginning reader has difficulty reading simple text.

## The Symptoms

Makes word errors, reads with choppy phrasing, and lacks expression

> **Kenny**, a beginning reader, had difficulty reading simple text. Though he was able to identify many sight words, he missed words he knew as he read. He read with a mixture of word-by-word and choppy phrasing and lacked expression.

## The Solution

Having students compose their own story about a familiar subject you've chosen allows beginning and struggling readers to read as the author. This perspective makes it easy for them to attach meaning to the text of the story and see the words on the page as a complete thought, rather than as individual parts.

> **Kenny** was given lots of practice reading the subject paragraphs he created. He loved writing about things familiar to him. Through this practice, he increased his ability to read with phrasing and expression, notably varying his tone to add emphasis to the story, which showed he understood what he read.

## Putting It to Work in Your Classroom

Use the Subject Paragraphs strategy with small groups of beginning and struggling readers who have similar needs. As children create subject paragraphs about their home and school experiences, help them make connections between their writing and the format, words, and style of other texts they encounter in the classroom.

## I. Preparing and Introducing the Activity

- Select a topic (see the Subject Paragraph Topics list on page 67).

- Introduce and discuss the paragraph topic to help children find words and ideas to use in their writing.

- Each day, have students select an aspect of their topic about which to write. For example, they might write a description of their family and then include a sentence about themselves, a sentence about each family member, a sentence about their pets, and so on. Have them write one or two sentences each day, depending on their writing abilities.

- Ask for the words students will want to use. For example, if the topic is "Me," they might give you the words *eyes, brown, blue, hair, black,* and *smile.* List these on the board or on a sheet of chart paper.

- Further assist students with their writing as needed. To scaffold the writing more intensively, you might prepare a paragraph with sentences partly completed (for example, *My name is _____. I like to play _____.*) and have students fill in one word in each sentence. If children are writing the paragraph on their own, you might have them write two or three sentences the first day and then add a few the next day and the following day to complete the paragraph.

Crystal Me
Me
I am a girl.
I am tall.
My eyes are dark bown.
My name is Crystal
I play by myself.
I am seven.
My birthday is in January.

Crystal wrote her subject paragraph about herself. She brainstormed what she would write with me and her peers and then wrote part of the paragraph one day and finished the next. She enjoyed reading it aloud in many contexts—at share time to the class, to other teachers, and to herself.

- When the children have completed all of the sentences, you may want them to illustrate the paragraph.

## 2. Modeling Fluent Oral Reading

- Read aloud each child's paragraph, attending to proper grouping and pausing at the end of every sentence.

## 3. Guiding Repeated Oral Reading

- If children are struggling with the words, have them read aloud the words on the board, repeating after you and then on their own.

- Listen to each child read his or her paragraph, helping him or her with phrasing and expression.

- Have children share their paragraphs, with different audiences reading them to you, to a partner, and to the group.

---

### Subject Paragraph Topics

**Me** What I look like, What I like to do, My best friend, My friends, What we like to play, Where I live

**My Family** Me, My mom, My dad, My grandpa [or other extended family members], My pet

**Our School** What the school looks like, Where the school is, My teachers, My ride to school, Our custodial staff, Our lunchroom, My principal, My media specialist, My teacher(s), What I am learning, My/Our classroom, My classmates, My favorite subject

---

## 4. Extending Repeated Oral Reading

*Sports Paragraphs* Encourage children who enjoy watching sports to write about big sports events, such as the World Series. Following a team with a small group of children who are sports enthusiasts can help them generate a tremendous amount of sight-word vocabulary and ideas to share in their writing. You might invite these children to become classroom sports announcers who read a one- or two-sentence team update to the class each day.

# LITERATURE RESPONSE STORIES

Children love to respond to favorite stories they've heard. This strategy invites struggling readers to respond to illustrations in books they've read. As they react to the illustrations, they identify new vocabulary that is meaningful to them and use concept words that were introduced to them through the read-aloud. They reinforce their word recognition and practice fluent phrasing as they reread and share stories they have written using the new vocabulary.

## The Problem

The struggling reader lacks appropriate phrasing and expression.

## The Symptoms

Reads slowly, grouping words in awkward phrasings; delivers a story with little expression

> **Kara**, a second grader, loved being read to and was eager to become a good reader. She listened intently when she was read to and joined wholeheartedly in the class discussions of the stories. When Kara read aloud, however, she read in a monotone voice and did not read words in meaningful units. She was unable to answer questions about what she had read.

## The Solution

Literature Response Stories is a strategy to help struggling readers read text with greater accuracy, rate, phrasing, expression, and prosody. Inviting children to actively respond to stories they hear during read-aloud time helps them approach new texts with the expectation that there will be something to respond to—and this expectation carries through in their delivery and expression as they read.

> **Kara** liked responding in writing to the literature read aloud to her and she liked reading her responses to others. When she combined what she had learned from hearing the story read fluently with her own retelling and response, her use of appropriate phrasing, expression, and prosody increased. With practice, she was able to transfer the fluency skills she had learned from reading her own writing to reading aloud other stories at her reading level.

## *Putting It to Work in Your Classroom*

Use Literature Response Stories with classes and small groups of children who have similar needs. Reading a picture book and providing the children with an illustration from the literature acts as a springboard to jump-start the children's writing (see Appendix C: Suggested Children's Literature for Building Fluency).

### I. Preparing and Introducing the Activity

- Select an engaging book to share with children and prepare an illustration sheet for the book.

- Read the book aloud to the group. Remember to hold the book so that all children can see it while you are reading.

- Discuss the story and include the questions "*Who is the story about?*" and "*What is the story about?*" Tell children they will retell the story or write about their favorite part to give other readers a review of the book.

- Ask them to give you the words they will need when they write their responses, and write these on the board or chart paper. Say them as you point to each one. (For example, words children might request for writing about *Franklin in the Dark* by Paulette Bourgeois might include *scared, dark, shell, monsters, night,* and *light.*)

- To assist children who are writing their own responses, you might provide them with the Picture Prompt Sheet on page 60. You may need to have children who require more support dictate part or all of their response to you.

Franklin *Vernon* the turtle.
Franklin was scared in his shell. His shell was to dark.
His mother was looking for him.
And his mother took him home. And has mother put a night light in his shell
He was scared of monsters.

This student responded to the book *Franklin in the Dark* by summarizing parts of the story.

## 2. Modeling Fluent Oral Reading

- Review the words children requested as needed, by reading aloud the words one at a time.

- Read each child's completed response story fluently.

## 3. Guiding Repeated Oral Reading

- Listen to the child read the story, helping him or her with phrasing and expression. Repeat as needed.

- Have children read their stories to one another and to the class.

## 4. Extending Repeated Oral Reading

***Response in Print*** Invite students to type and print their responses to literature on the computer and practice reading them fluently to you or a partner. Display students' writing in the classroom for others to read and let children take a copy home to read to a family member.

***Response Journal Writing*** Have children keep a notebook in which they reread their responses to books they have read independently, writing retellings or commenting on a favorite part or a character. Have them write the book's title and author and the date of their response for each entry. Be sure to have them practice reading their literature responses to partners or, alternatively, to the class. Make it a goal to have struggling readers read you their written responses once a week so you can monitor their expression and phrasing.

# RECORDED REPEATED READING 🔍 ✢ 🕐 🎼 🎭

**R**ecorded reading is a valuable way to provide students with repeated reading practice and is one of the quickest ways to increase a struggling reader's fluency. Recording his or her own voice reading helps the child self-monitor and self-correct and boosts his or her confidence in reading—a big motivator for struggling readers. With this strategy, the struggling reader can practice reading texts that others in the class are reading with ease until he or she, too, can read it smoothly.

### The Problem

The struggling reader reads too slowly or too fast and lacks confidence.

### The Symptoms

Makes multiple word recognition errors and lacks appropriate phrasing and expression; or reads too fast, ignoring punctuation, and lacks appropriate phrasing and expression

> **John**, a second grader, lacked confidence in his reading yet wanted to be able to read fluently for his mother the way his younger sister did. He read very slowly with choppy phrasing. He was unable to recognize many words, and because he always made mistakes when he read aloud he was embarrassed by his reading.

### The Solution

Recorded Repeated Reading helps struggling readers to read text accurately with appropriate rate, phrasing, and expression. The strategy is simple and easy for children to use independently: They record, listen to, and re-record their oral reading of the same paragraph until they are satisfied with their performance.

> **John** simply needed to practice his reading aloud with some guidance. I gave him a short paragraph from his grade-level reading text and read the passage fluently for him. Then I had him read through the paragraph and helped him with unknown words and with his phrasing and expression. I set him up with a tape recorder and blank tape and showed him how to record himself. John recorded and re-recorded his oral reading of the same paragraph for 15 minutes, until he liked the way he sounded. Then he read the paragraph to me and to his teacher, making only two errors. He could already taste success. "This is the first time I will be able to read to my mother without making a whole lot of mistakes," he announced. This became a great fluency-building activity for John, who was eager to challenge himself and work independently with new passages.

### *Putting It to Work in Your Classroom*

Use Recorded Repeated Reading with individuals or small groups of struggling readers. You will need to set up a recording/listening center and provide children with a paragraph to practice reading. For example, you might select a paragraph from the reading selection you are working on in class. Allow a child 10–15 minutes to record and re-record his or her oral reading of the paragraph. Then have the child read the passage aloud to you.

You may wish to use this strategy with your group divided into three smaller groups and have them rotate as follows: one group at the reading/recording/listening center practicing a fluent reading of a passage independently, one group receiving teacher-directed instruction (providing phrasing tips on a child's oral reading, building vocabulary, or using another activity to support fluency), and one group practicing their reading in pairs.

### I. Preparing and Introducing the Activity

- Prepare the recording/listening center. Have one tape available for each child to use. Mark children's names on the tapes and place them in a basket to keep the center organized.

- Select a paragraph for which the child has learned the vocabulary. The child should have read the paragraph but should not be able to read it fluently. The child may read from a copy of the paragraph or directly from the text.

> For the child who reads too rapidly with inappropriate phrasing and inattention to punctuation, put a slash mark after each phrase in the text. Have him or her group together the words within the slash marks, pausing briefly at the end slash mark before reading the next group of words.

### 2. Modeling Fluent Oral Reading

- Read the passage aloud fluently for the child.

## 3. Guiding Repeated Oral Reading

- Ask the child to read the paragraph silently and then to read it aloud to you. Assist him or her with the words and with his or her phrasing and expression as needed.

> Remind children to observe punctuation as they read. For example, you might tell them that a period marks the end of a thought, and a reader must take a breath before reading on.

- Have the child record, listen to, and re-record his or her oral reading of the paragraph, until he or she is able to read the text quickly and accurately with appropriate phrasing and expression and is satisfied with the fluency.

- Have the child read the passage to you. Praise his or her effort and make specific suggestions for improving the next reading, such as making sure his or her voice rises at the end of a question (inflection). If you do not have time to listen and respond to each child during the course of your instruction time, encourage the student to read the passage to a classmate. Listen to his or her taped reading later in the day and provide feedback on a sticky note for the child to read the next day.

- If the child needs more practice, you may wish to fluently read the passage aloud to the child again. Have the child read it after you, making sure he or she takes a breath when he or she comes to a slash, comma, or sentence end mark.

## 4. Extending Repeated Oral Reading

***Select and Share*** Invite struggling readers to select a passage from a story or nonfiction passage they have read. Challenge children to practice reading and recording the passage smoothly and clearly with expression until they have a recording with which they are satisfied. Let children then read the passage to another staff member in the school.

***Before and After*** Have struggling readers make two recordings of the passage, a "Before" recording before practicing, and an "After" recording when they've worked on the passage awhile. Let them take the tapes home or invite parents to listen during parent-teacher conferences. Note specific areas of improvement evident on the recording, such as word recognition, phrasing, and expression.

# UNTIMED REPEATED READING 🔍 ✢ 🕐 🎼 🎭

**T**oo many times, teachers present a reading lesson and then move on to the next one before many of their students have learned to read the lesson text comfortably. Yet struggling readers need repeated exposure to and practice with the text to build accuracy and proficiency. This strategy helps meet the individual needs of struggling readers and to involve their family members in building literacy as well. It works even with families who have limited time and resources—the child brings home only passages that he or she has practiced and can read accurately with correct phrasing and expression, so that any family member can listen to the child read, if nothing else. Reading the story or passage multiple times in different contexts (school and home) improves the child's reading tremendously.

### The Problem

The struggling reader reads below grade level and with little confidence.

### The Symptoms

Reads too slowly with word recognition errors; lacks expression; ignores punctuation; lacks confidence in own reading

> **Sammy**, a third grader who was reading below grade level, was embarrassed by his inability to read aloud fluently. When he read aloud, he usually missed words, ignored punctuation, and read very slowly.

### The Solution

The Untimed Repeated Reading strategy enables beginning and struggling readers to increase their fluency and to read aloud with accuracy, appropriate phrasing, and expression. You might use this strategy three to four days a week until the student is able to read a paragraph aloud quickly and accurately with ease and confidence.

> **Sammy**'s grandmother had the time to listen to him read. So every day I provided Sammy with a new paragraph and helped him practice reading it several times. Then he took the paragraph home, read it aloud five times to his grandmother, and the next day he read it fluently to me. At first he practiced reading paragraphs at his instructional reading level, but as his fluency increased, I gave him paragraphs from our third-grade reader. Sammy was proud of his improvement in fluency and in his ability to fluently read grade-level text. As Sammy's fluency increased, his classroom performance improved as well, and he participated more frequently.

### *Putting It to Work in Your Classroom*

Use Untimed Repeated Reading with individual readers. Begin by giving the child a short selection to practice reading that is at his or her instructional level. Make sure the child is familiar with the vocabulary. As the child becomes more fluent in his or her reading, gradually assign more text. Giving the child a longer paragraph or moving from one to two or three paragraphs increases the amount of sustained reading time the reader has to practice a single passage. This helps the child develop a sense of flow in his or her reading and enables the child to perceive more easily the sentences in the paragraphs as a series of connected ideas.

### I. Preparing and Introducing the Activity

- Select a passage the child has read before and for which he or she has learned the vocabulary. The child may read from a copy of the passage or directly from a text he or she can take home.

### 2. Modeling Fluent Oral Reading

- Read the passage aloud fluently for the child using appropriate rate, accuracy, and expression.

### 3. Guiding Repeated Oral Reading

- Help the child read the passage for or with you to ensure his or her accurate word recognition and to guide his attention to punctuation, phrasing, and expression. If the child misses any words, pronounce them correctly and have him or her reread the sentences with the missed words.

- Have the child read the entire passage orally to you several times until he is able to read it fairly fluently.

- Have the child take the passage home to read at least five times to a family member. Ask the family member to sign the passage with his or her name and the date or send a note indicating that the child has completed the readings.

- The next day, listen to the child read the passage and provide positive, encouraging feedback. Make note of his or her ability to phrase appropriately. Also note the rate of the reading, which should increase with practice as the child learns to anticipate the words and ideas in the passage.

- As the child gains fluency, you may want to increase not only the length but also the difficulty of the text. As with the Recorded Repeated Reading strategy, if the child is unable to handle the passage, go back to a more comfortable reading level and try a longer or more difficult text again later.

## 4. Extending Repeated Oral Reading

*My Choice Reading* Allow the child to select and practice reading a paragraph or passage of his or her own choosing from a text in the classroom. Encourage the child to choose a passage that he or she would want to share with someone, such as an informational paragraph about the solar system with facts about the sizes of the planets. Make sure the passage comes from a text he or she has previously read. First have the child read the passage to you or a partner who will offer guidance. Then have the child practice reading it to a family member or a partner. When he or she is ready, ask the child to read the practiced passage to you. The child may also record his or her reading of the passage at a recording/listening center before taking it home to read (see Recorded Repeated Reading, pages 71–73).

## CHAPTER 4

# Expression and Prosody

**A**n effective read-aloud moves the listener—the reader relays lines of dialogue in an argument as if the words had sharp edges; brings a hushed tone of seriousness to a news report about a natural disaster; makes a dramatic pause before revealing the identity of the thief at the end of a mystery. Fluent readers select from a toolbox of prosodic and expressive aids: tempo, rhythm, pitch, voice level, and phrasing to understand and communicate what they read.

The strategies in this chapter help children build their fluency skills and improve their comprehension as they practice reading aloud to interpret text and reflect the author's tone, mood, and intent. The ability to capture a listener's attention with an expressive reading is highly motivating to struggling readers. I find these strategies to be some of the most engaging and rewarding for these students.

# TEACHER READ-ALOUD WITH MULTIPLE COPIES

Read-alouds offer a highly motivating purpose for struggling readers to practice reading—they want to read what you've read with the same enthusiasm and expression. This strategy helps students practice intonation, phrasing, and using expression to convey mood as they reread and interpret a meaningful text.

## The Problem

The struggling, unmotivated reader lacks expression and prosody.

## The Symptoms

Has poor word recognition, reads too slowly with incorrect phrasing and in a monotone, and lacks motivation to read; or reads words rapidly with incorrect punctuation and phrasing; does not attempt to read books on own

> **Tanya**, a first grader, loved books and showed a great interest in reading. She loved being read to and was an enthusiastic participant in the class discussions of the stories. Her own reading, however, was fraught with difficulty, and she stumbled through text, missing words and reading without expression. This made it difficult for others to listen to her when she read.

## The Solution

Hearing good literature read fluently and expressively motivates children to practice reading the same text. When you use this strategy regularly with struggling readers, they soon begin asking for copies of your read-aloud books as soon as you've finished reading. Encourage them to pick up and read books on their own.

> Each day, I read aloud a book to **Tanya's** class as they were gathered around me on the rug. For this strategy I chose books I love to read, like *The Little Engine That Could*, so that I would read as expressively as possible. This gave Tanya and her peers the opportunity to hear the text read with appropriate phrasing and expression. Afterward, Tanya practiced reading the book with a partner. She was thrilled as her peers began to notice how well she was able to "act out" the stories with her voice. This strategy was key to her becoming an avid, expressive, fluent reader.

### Putting It to Work in Your Classroom

Use Teacher Read-Aloud With Multiple Copies with classes and small groups of struggling readers who have similar needs. Select a variety of sight-word books, easy-to-read books, and books with dialogue-rich text of which you can obtain multiple copies or book sets (see Appendix C: Suggested Children's Literature for Building Fluency). Make sure that the books also contain words children are learning in class (or add these words to your list before introducing a book). To build excitement about and familiarity with the featured text, read the book to the children more than once during the week. Display the multiple copies on the chalkboard tray and in other prominent places in the room so that children notice them and have easy access to them.

### I. Preparing and Introducing the Activity

- Gather multiple copies of the book.

- Read through the book to plan how you will orally interpret the text and to identify key concept words that you want children to know.

- Discuss briefly with children, before and during reading, the meanings of key concept words and phrases or expressions essential to understanding the story.

### 2. Modeling Fluent Oral Reading

- Read aloud the book fluently to children. Present the story in a meaningful way through phrasing, intonation, stress, rhythm, pitch, and so on. Hold the picture book to one side of you with the pictures facing the group and turn the pages so children can see the pictures and text as you read.

- After discussing the story, point out the text's prosodic features and typographical markings, such as punctuation marks, large bold print, underlining, and italics, that guide expressive reading. Read aloud selections with examples of these features and ask children how the features help you read expressively.

- Read the book again to the children during the week.

> Using a Big Book will make it easier to call the children's attention to typographical markings, which serve as guideposts for reading expressively.

### 3. Guiding Repeated Oral Reading

- Give the children a copy of the book. If you have more children than you have book copies, put out the multiple copies of the previous week's feature book, too. Let children take turns with the books.

- Ask children to read through the book once, asking you or a partner for help with any unfamiliar words.

- Have students read the book with a partner. Listen to their reading and provide suggestions for improving their phrasing and expression, pointing out contextual and typographical cues. Reread sections fluently for those children who need extra support.

### 4. Extending Repeated Oral Reading

*Poem Time* Plan a time each week to read aloud poetry and rhymes to your class or to a small group and provide the children with copies of the poems. Have students practice reading the poetry and rhymes with partners and in small groups and invite them to perform their poems chorally or in parts for the class at the end of the week. Let children compile their copies into a book that they can read aloud in other school settings and at home.

*Cliff-Hanger Reading* Leave students wondering. Read a simple chapter book that struggling readers will be able to handle and stop at a particularly exciting part. Students will want to know what happened next and will continue reading the book on their own. Many of the children I've taught began reading chapter books on their own with this encouragement. Ask students periodically to read a favorite part to you so you can monitor their fluency and interpretation.

# DIALOGUE THEATER 

Just as students love to respond to favorite read-aloud literature in writing (see Literature Response Stories on pages 68–70), they also love to enact these stories. Dialogue Theater scripts make great fluency-building materials that engage students in repeated reading for a purpose: to practice expressively reading the dialogue they enjoyed listening to in the read-aloud. The simplified Dialogue Theater script contains sight and vocabulary words students recognize from the literature, which students will practice reading repeatedly as they rehearse. Children tend to get so involved in learning to read their parts well that they never mind practicing the parts over and over, thus increasing their accuracy, rate, phrasing, and expression.

## The Problem

The struggling unfocused reader has little motivation to read.

## The Symptoms

Reads too slowly, with inappropriate rate, phrasing, and expression, and lacks appropriate oral interpretation; or reads too rapidly and lacks expression

> **Toby**, a first grader, had a sense of humor and a ready grin. But he was a disfluent reader with limited sight vocabulary and he read with a lack of expression. Unable to sit for long, Toby was constantly up and down and it was a struggle to get him to focus on his work. He liked being the center of attention and created daily disturbances in class.

## The Solution

Dialogue Theater helps struggling readers to focus on the meaning of a text and improve their oral interpretation skills. It works particularly well with children who thrive on interaction and attention.

> **Toby** was a natural for theater. He loved read-aloud stories with funny problems and dialogue. His favorite book was *The Little Red Hen*. He loved hearing the story over and over and repeating the words as I read them: "'Not I,' said the cat, 'Not I,' said the rat, 'Not I,' said the dog." Toby loved practicing his favorite lines from the scripts I created and adding gestures and movements. When he fluently performed his part, he glowed with pride.

### Putting It to Work in Your Classroom

Use Dialogue Theater with classes of struggling readers who have similar needs. I find the scripts that work best come from stories and books with lots of dialogue and predictable repetitive phrases, lines, or sentences, such as *The Little Red Hen* ("'Not I,' said the pig"), *The Three Billy Goats Gruff* ("Trip trap, Trip, trap"), and *The Three Little Pigs* ("'Not by the hair of my chinny chin chin'"). I also look for a story problem that provides opportunities for reading with expression. Encourage children to add movements to their performance and allow those who need lots of movement to act out their parts.

On pages 84–89, you'll find scripts that I have written for my struggling beginning readers. These scripts use sight words and simple text to tell the story of *The Little Red Hen* and two stories based on *Caps for Sale* by Esphyr Slobodkina: *Trees for Sale* and *Three Homes for Three Puppies.*

### I. Preparing and Introducing the Activity

- Select a story or scene from a favorite read-aloud book that contains a lot of dialogue. (Make sure that you recently have read the book to the class or to a small group of struggling readers.)

- Discuss with children how the voices of the characters should be performed (orally interpreted) before you have them work with the script. For example, you might ask how the children will read animal noises or the voice of a worried mother.

- Prepare a script that uses sight words that students have encountered.

- Write the lines of dialogue in simple sentences that your readers can handle without experiencing frustration.

- Make copies of the script for the group and distribute.

- List words that may give your students trouble.

- Review the words, saying the words and pointing to them.

- Assign the script parts. Two or more children may be assigned to each of the parts, and the parts can be read chorally.

> You can change the number of characters in the script, depending on the number of parts needed. To create more parts, I sometimes split a single part into two, or have several students read the part of the narrator or chorus; to create fewer parts, I stick with the most important characters and have them explain or summarize the parts that I've cut.

## 2. Modeling Fluent Oral Reading

- Read aloud the script fluently with children reading along in their scripts.

- Read the script fluently a second time, emphasizing the appropriate expression that each character's lines and personality suggest. Demonstrate how the mood or tone of the scene determines how you interpret the lines with your voice (for example, you might show frustration as you read the part of the Little Red Hen, who is left to do all the work while the other animals won't help her but want to eat the bread).

## 3. Guiding Repeated Oral Reading

- Have children read through the script until they can read their parts fluently with appropriate phrasing and expression. Encourage students to use appropriate movements, gestures, and facial expressions to convey the appropriate tone and feelings intended by the author.

- When children can read their parts well, have them perform the script for the class. For students who need to move, encourage them to keep their gestures simple so they can also deliver their lines.

## 4. Extending Repeated Oral Reading

*Compare-and-Contrast Group Dialogue Theater* Assign the same script to several small groups. Provide minimal guidance, encouraging each group to interpret the script. Have the groups practice reading their parts and then perform the script. In a class discussion, compare and contrast the different ways each of the groups approached the task, their oral interpretations, and the merits of each.

*Book Conversations* Perform Dialogue Theater with conversations read directly from the text. Have children pair up and read conversations between two characters, such as Frog and Toad in *Frog and Toad Are Friends* by Arnold Lobel, and from memorable scenes, such as those in *Charlotte's Web* when Fern pleads with her father for Wilbur's life and when Avery finds out his sister Fern has a pig.

As they practice their lines, remind children to reread the text from which the script was written so they can better understand the dialogue in context.

Name _____ Date_____

# The Little Red Hen
## Dialogue Theater

**THE CHARACTERS**
Narrator     Little Red Hen     Cat     Dog     Pig

**Narrator:**     One day Little Red Hen found some seeds.
**Little Red Hen:**     Who will help me plant the seeds?
**Cat:**     Meow, meow! Not I!
**Dog:**     Woof, woof! Not I!
**Pig:**     Oink, oink! Not I!
**Little Red Hen:**     Then I will do it myself.
**Narrator:**     And she did.

**Little Red Hen:**     Who will help me cut this wheat?
**Cat:**     Meow, meow! Not I!
**Dog:**     Woof, woof! Not I!
**Pig:**     Oink, oink! Not I!
**Little Red Hen:**     Then I will do it myself.
**Narrator:**     And she did.

**Little Red Hen:**     Who will help me take this to the mill?
**Cat:**     Meow, meow! Not I!
**Dog:**     Woof, woof! Not I!
**Pig:**     Oink, oink! Not I!
**Little Red Hen:**     Then I will do it myself.
**Narrator:**     And she did.

Name _____ Date_____

# The Little Red Hen
## Dialogue Theater (continued)

| | |
|---|---|
| **Little Red Hen:** | Who will help me bake the bread? |
| **Cat:** | Meow, meow! Not I! |
| **Dog:** | Woof, woof! Not I! |
| **Pig:** | Oink, oink! Not I! |
| **Little Red Hen:** | Then I will do it myself. |
| **Narrator:** | And she did. |
| | |
| **Little Red Hen:** | Who will help me eat this bread? |
| **Cat:** | Meow, meow! I will! |
| **Dog:** | Woof, woof! I will! |
| **Pig:** | Oink, oink! I will! |
| **Little Red Hen:** | No, you will not. I will eat it myself! |
| | |
| **Narrator:** | And she did! |

Name _____ Date_____

# Trees for Sale
## Dialogue Theater

> **READING PARTS**
> Readers 1, 2, 3, 4, 5, 6

**Reader 1:**    We have **four** trees. We must sell the trees.

**Reader 2:**    I know how to sell the trees. We will sell them in town.

**Reader 3:**    Trees for sale! Four trees for sale!

**Reader 4:**    May I buy a tree, please? I want a big tree.

**Reader 1:**    Yes. You may buy a tree. Here is a big tree.

**Reader 2:**    Now we need to sell **three** trees.

**Reader 3:**    Trees for sale! Three trees for sale!

**Reader 5:**    May I buy a tree? I want a little tree.

**Reader 1:**    Yes. You may buy a tree. Here is a little tree.

Name _____ Date_____

# Trees for Sale
## Dialogue Theater (continued)

**Reader 2:**    Now we need to sell **two** trees.

**Reader 3:**    Trees for sale! Two trees for sale!

**Reader 6:**    May I buy a tree? I want a tall tree.

**Reader 1:**    Yes. You may buy a tree. Here is a tall tree.


**Reader 2:**    Now we need to sell **one** tree.

**Reader 3:**    I have an idea. Let's keep this tree. We will plant it at home.

**Readers 1, 2, 3:**  Yes, let's!

# Three Homes for Three Puppies
## Dialogue Theater

> **READING PARTS**
> Readers 1, 2, 3, 4, 5, 6

**Reader 1:** Our dog Daisy has three puppies.
Daisy has a black puppy,
a brown puppy,
and a black and brown
and tan puppy.

**Reader 2:** We must find homes
for Daisy's puppies.
We must find a good home
for each puppy.
We will need **three** homes
for **three** puppies.

**Reader 1:** I know how to find homes
for the puppies.
I will find three good homes
for Daisy's puppies.

**Reader 2:** Puppies for free!
Three free puppies!

**Reader 3:** Let's see the puppies.
Can we keep the black puppy, please?

Name _____ Date_____

# Three Homes for Three Puppies
## Dialogue Theater (continued)

**Reader 4:**     Yes. We can keep the black puppy.

**Reader 1:**     Now we need **two** homes
for **two** puppies.

**Reader 2:**     Puppies for free!
Two free puppies!

**Reader 5:**     Let's see the puppies.
Can we keep the brown puppy, please?

**Reader 6:**     Yes. We can keep the brown puppy.

**Reader 1:**     Now we need **one** home
for **one** puppy,
a black and brown and tan puppy.
We must find a good home
for this puppy.

**Reader 2:**     I know a good home
for this puppy.
We can keep this black and brown
and tan puppy!

**Readers 1, 2:**   This puppy will have a good home
with us and Daisy!

# CROSS-AGE REPEATED READING 🔍 ✦ 🎼 🎭 ✷

**O**lder readers who have struggled with their reading for several years often need reasons to read. When you ask them to read to a younger child who needs help learning to read, you provide them with a true purpose for improving their own oral reading fluency. They also gain confidence as they begin to make a difference in another child's life. This strategy proves to be very effective with students who exhibit behavior problems and lack confidence in their abilities.

### The Problem

The struggling, older reader lacks motivation for repeated reading practice.

### The Symptoms

Reads word by word with choppy phrasing and a lack of accuracy; reads in a monotone; does not like to reread text

> **Melvin**, a third grader, was a tall, often belligerent student who had already been retained and was reading at a beginning second-grade level. He rarely attended to his work and disliked reading; as a consequence, he frequently disrupted the classroom by bothering other children.

### The Solution

Cross-Age Repeated Reading helps motivate reluctant second and third graders who are reading below grade level to read and reread for fluency. Struggling readers often become great mentors and role models as they support younger peers—meanwhile, they build fluency skills by modeling good oral reading.

> I paired **Melvin** with a beginning first-grade reader, and then later, at his request, with a group of three children. He was tremendously proud of his ability to read to the younger children. He mirrored many of the techniques I used when I read aloud to him and he noticed how building background and reviewing unfamiliar words with "his" students helped them read better. Melvin's reading improved tremendously as he continued to mentor—so did his attitude toward reading!

### Putting It to Work in Your Classroom

Use Cross-Age Repeated Reading with individuals or small groups of older struggling readers who have similar needs. The strategy provides children with a purpose for the repeated reading of appropriately leveled text. Find a first-grade teacher in your school who has struggling readers and is willing to participate.

## 1. Preparing and Introducing the Activity

- Working with a first-grade teacher, partner one of your struggling readers with a first-grade struggling reader. Consider abilities, personalities, interests, and gender as you match children.

- Prepare a schedule for the children to read together once or twice a week.

- Help your reader select a book appropriate to his or her own reading level as well as the age and interests of the first-grade partner. Make sure that both partners can handle the length of the book.

## 2. Modeling Fluent Oral Reading

- Read the selected book aloud fluently to the older reader.

## 3. Guiding Repeated Oral Reading

- Have your student read the book to you, helping him or her with any unfamiliar or difficult words. Give the child time to practice reading the book aloud to a partner until he or she is able to read it with appropriate expression, rate, and accuracy. Or you may want to have the child practice the read-aloud using the Recorded Repeated Reading strategy (pages 71–73).

- Supervise or train a reliable classroom volunteer to supervise the partner reading. Note how the older reader presents the book to the younger child and how the younger child receives it. After each session, based on what you observe, provide the older reader with one or two helpful tips (for example, remind the student to pause at end marks and to make the dialogue sound like a real conversation). Be sure to offer lots of encouragement.

## 4. Extending Repeated Oral Reading

*Cross-Age Dialogue Theater* Write a script based on a favorite book that several partners have shared or select another script that will appeal to both the older and younger readers. Assign the older and younger students parts in the script. Have students practice their parts together and then perform for another class of first graders. (See the Dialogue Theater strategy, pages 81–89.)

---

Encouraging the older readers to return to the text from which the script was written can help them see the dialogue again in the context of the story, and thereby better understand characters' feelings and motives. This will help them add expression to their reading of the script.

---

# THE INTERVIEW STRATEGY 🔍 ✦ 🕐 🎼 🎭 ✹

**H**aving struggling readers conduct interviews with adults helps them build fluency and gain knowledge about careers and jobs. Children enjoy generating questions, asking the questions during the interview, and reading the completed interview transcripts. This strategy encourages them to engage in repeated reading, providing lots of opportunities to write, recognize, and read many of the same words across the different interviews they conduct.

## The Problem

The unmotivated student reads below grade level.

## The Symptoms

Unable to read with appropriate phrasing and expression and lacks motivation for repeated reading practice; or reads too fast without meaningful phrasing and expression

> **Joseph**, a third grader, had a great deal of difficulty reading and received little support at home for improvement. He stumbled slowly through text, reading with choppy phrasing and a lack of expression. He did not like to read.

## The Solution

The Interview Strategy can be used to motivate small groups of struggling readers to practice repeated readings of texts that they have helped to author.

> **Joseph** loved interviewing the school staff and the visitors we had. He was diligent in writing and practicing his interview questions so that he could fluently deliver them. I compiled Joseph's and his classmates' interview questions, the transcribed responses, and the photos I took of the interviews and published them in a booklet. The booklet served as a nonfiction text for Joseph and his classmates to read in class and at home.

## Putting It to Work in Your Classroom

Use the Interview Strategy with classes and small groups of struggling readers who have similar needs. Arrange for students to interview school staff such as the principal, custodian, and librarian. You may also want to invite local professionals, such as artists, construction workers, or people in business or medicine, to be interviewed by the whole class. Another good source for interesting interviewees may be a field trip to a local business, which allows children to interview people on the job.

> I find that learning to fluently read their questions and their interviewee's answers provides children with such valuable and enjoyable repeated reading practice that I have students interview many different people over the course of a year. I compile the children's interviews into class booklets for them to practice reading in class and at home.

## I. Preparing and Introducing the Activity

- Select a person to interview, obtain their consent, and set an interview date. Ask the interviewee to plan on keeping his or her answers fairly short (roughly one to three sentences) so that children can understand and record answers.

- Two days prior to the interview, build background with children about interviewing professional people; make sure they understand that in an interview they can expect to find out about the interviewee's job, family, and what they like to do in their free time. Ask children to share what they know about interviews they may have seen on TV. Let children view or read a short interview. (An easy way to prepare an interview model is to conduct a three- to four-question interview with a willing teaching colleague whom the children know well and then transcribe the interview onto chart paper.)

- A day before the interview, tell the class whom the visiting interviewee will be and have children share what they know about his or her job. Ask children what they would like to know about the interviewee and list or make a web of their ideas on the board or overhead (number of children, hobbies or interests, job title, favorite parts of their job, least favorite parts of the job, job training, and so on). For example, to prepare for an interview with a zookeeper, I used the categories my students brainstormed to create this web:

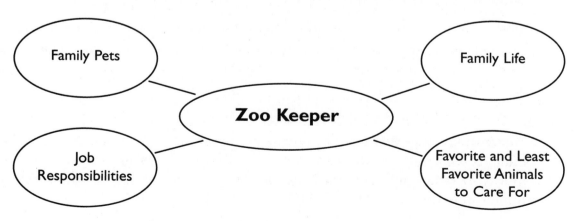

- Using an overhead transparency of the Zookeeper Interview on page 95, show children a model class interview.

- Help students generate and write two to five interview questions each, using their categories and the other interviews they've heard or read as a guide. Make sure students understand that some questions may not be appropriate in an interview. (For example, it's usually not a good idea to ask interviewees their age, but asking them how old they were when they began training for their job is fine.)

- Help each child read aloud one or two of their questions and select or have the class decide on four to six of these questions. Write the questions on the board or a sheet of chart paper.

- Read the questions aloud, showing children how to use appropriate inflection when asking a question in a polite manner.

- Help children prepare and practice for the interview by reading aloud the questions with a partner.

- Conduct the interview. Let individuals or small groups ask the questions. Record the interview and take photographs.

- Later, transcribe the interviewee's answers, simplifying his or her responses as needed.

- Make copies of the transcription and distribute to children.

## 2. Modeling Fluent Oral Reading

- Read aloud the questions and answers from the interview transcript fluently, emphasizing appropriate phrasing and expression.

## 3. Guiding Repeated Oral Reading

- Group children in pairs and ask them to take on the roles of interviewer and interviewee. Have one partner read the questions and the other read the answers. Then have them switch roles and read the interview again. As students practice, provide them with suggestions for improving their phrasing and expression.

## 4. Extending Repeated Oral Reading

- *Student-Selected Group Interviews* When children have practiced the strategy once or twice, encourage a small group to select a person they want to interview. Offer the group assistance in arranging, recording, and transcribing the interview.

Name _____ Date_____

# Zookeeper Interview

**Question 1:**     What do you do at the zoo?

**Answer:**     I am a zookeeper and I work with the mammals.

**Question 2:**     Do you like working at the zoo?

**Answer:**     Yes, I like working at the zoo because I like working with animals. I even like the reptiles. My favorite one is the boa constrictor.

**Question 3:**     How many animals do you care for?

**Answer:**     I help with all of the animals wherever I'm needed.

**Question 4:**     How did you learn to take care of the animals at the zoo?

**Answer:**     First I was a zookeeper's assistant at another zoo. Then, when I came to this zoo, I had special training by other zookeepers.

Name _____ Date_____

# Zookeeper Interview (continued)

**Question 5:**     How do you know what to feed the animals?

**Answer:**     A zoo dietician and a veterinarian tell us what to feed each animal. They know how much and what kind of food the animals will eat every day.

**Question 6:**     Is it hard work taking care of the animals?

**Answer:**     Sometimes it's fun and sometimes it's hard work. It's fun when I get to bring an animal to the vet for a checkup. Other parts are not so much fun. Cleaning the cages is hard work.

# CHAPTER 5

# Assessing Fluency

Some struggling readers exhibit just one disfluency symptom: getting stuck on multisyllabic words, or reading in a monotone, or stumbling through text in a halting, disjointed manner. However, most struggling readers experience a combination of disfluency symptoms. Given the importance of fluency to a reader's comprehension and the range of fluency skills readers must master—from decoding to expression—it's critically important that our assessment and instruction target the specific fluency elements that will best help a reader attain grade-level fluency.

**A THOROUGH ASSESSMENT MUST DETERMINE A READER'S ABILITY TO:**

- pace him- or herself when reading. Is the child's reading rate too slow or too quick to make his or her delivery meaningful?

- recognize and decode. Is the child able to immediately recognize sight words and to sound out unknown words without getting stuck or missing important information as he or she reads?

- phrase appropriately. Can the child group written words together in meaningful chunks, the way the words would be spoken?

- deliver the text expressively. Do the child's voice, face, and gestures carry the intent or emotional texture intended by the author?

- read prosodically. Does the child effectively use elements such as tempo, pitch, volume, and rhythm to follow punctuation marks and other typographical elements in the text?

In addition to using a baseline assessment that helps us determine areas for targeted instruction, we need to monitor the progress of our struggling readers carefully and frequently. Given our limited time as classroom teachers, the assessment tools we use for individual readers must be simple and quick to administer. This chapter describes assessment tools that meet these criteria and help you keep track of the progress of each struggling reader throughout the year.

# *Appropriate Assessment for Fluency*

## FIRST GRADE

First-grade struggling readers will not be ready for a passage-based fluency assessment until they are reading connected text. However, exposure to and practice with connected text in the form of two- to four-word sentences can begin immediately, even as readers are still learning letter sounds. As the lessons in Chapters 1 and 2 recommend, you can create simple sentences and stories in which sight words or words with target sounds appear and have children practice reading and re-creating those sentences with letter cards and in writing. Listen to the quality of children's oral reading as they practice with these and other texts, and use the strategies from Chapters 3 and 4 in this book to ensure the children are developing the use of appropriate phrasing and expression.

Often teachers are very concerned with struggling readers' pace or rate of reading. According to the fluency norms adapted by Rasinski (2003b) from Hasbrouck & Tindal (1992) and Howe & Shinn (2001), by the end of first grade, children should be reading 60 words correct per minute (wcpm) in a grade-level passage. This is a good indicator of whether a reader can process text at an appropriate rate. While the assessment tools I recommend in this chapter do measure reading rate, I do not use isolated strategies to help young children improve their reading rate; a child's reading rate will naturally increase as his or her skills in accuracy, decoding, phrasing, and expression increase.

As Tim Rasinski reminds us (2003a), focusing reading instruction exclusively on improving children's rate of reading will most likely help children read faster, but with little comprehension. Recently I worked with a group of primary-grade teachers who had been focusing solely on helping their students read text quickly and had been surprised by the low comprehension scores of their students whose reading rates had improved dramatically. I showed them how to integrate strategies from Chapters 3 and 4 into their instruction so they could build in time for students to practice phrasing, expression, and retelling. Their students are now making gains in comprehension in tandem with their improved rate.

## Second and Third Grade

Individually assess second- and third-grade struggling readers' fluency at the beginning of the school year, at midyear, and at the end of the year using a passage-based fluency assessment tool such as the Individual Oral Reading Fluency Assessment described on the following pages. Taken at the beginning of the year, the fluency assessment provides you with baseline data that highlights specific challenges facing the reader and helps you determine the appropriate instruction he or she needs to gain fluency. Taken in the middle of the year, this assessment allows you to note areas of progress and adjust your instruction as needed—perhaps a shift in focus from recognizing and decoding to phrasing. And at the end of the year, a final assessment helps you evaluate the effectiveness of your instruction and make recommendations for continued fluency support over the summer and into the next school year.

A child's reading rate increases as his or her ability to handle increasingly challenging texts increases. According to Rasinski's fluency norms, second graders should be reading grade-level text at a rate of 53 wcpm at the beginning of the school year, 78 wcpm by the middle of the year, and 94 wcpm by the end of the year. According to the same norms, third graders should be reading grade-level text at a rate of 79 wcpm at the beginning of the school year, 93 wcpm by the middle of the year, and 114 wcpm by the end of the year. Remember that as children gain skills in their target areas, their rate will automatically improve.

As an alternative to the assessment tools presented here, you may want to assess children's fluency using commercially published fluency assessments such as *Dynamic Indicators of Basic Early Literacy Skills* (Good & Kaminski, 2002), *3-Minute Reading Assessments* (Rasinski & Padak, 2005), or the assessment tools provided by your school district or reading basal. Review the components listed in the Individual Oral Reading Fluency Assessment (pages 101–103), the Oral Reading Quality Scale (page 108), and the Retelling Comprehension Rubric (page 109) to make sure the assessment you choose covers elements of rate and accuracy, quality, and retelling.

# *Individual Oral Reading Fluency Assessment*

Over the course of the last two years, my colleague Patsy Capps and I have developed a short individual assessment that provides teachers with a snapshot of their struggling readers' fluency strengths and weaknesses. Administered at least three times over the course of the year, it measures a student's oral reading fluency rate and word recognition accuracy by determining how many correct words the child can read in a grade-level passage in one minute. We also look at the percentage of words the child accurately recognizes.

We assess rate and decoding in tandem with two other fluency elements: the quality of oral reading and the quality of the retelling or summarizing of what has been read. The tools we've adapted include the Oral Reading Quality Scale, a qualitative assessment of phrasing, expression, and prosody that rates the child's oral reading performance (page 108) and the Retelling Comprehension Rubric, a guideline for evaluating the completeness and sequence of a retelling (page 109). In all, the full assessment and evaluation takes about three to four minutes, which enables you to meet with and assess several struggling readers over the course of an independent work period.

An explanation of how to use these tools and keep track of progress on the Fluency Assessment Record (page 110) follows.

## ADMINISTERING THE INDIVIDUAL ORAL READING FLUENCY ASSESSMENT

Following are some simple procedures to use when assessing children's oral reading fluency. If you have not done this type of assessment before, you'll want to practice giving the assessment to a child in your family or practice with a colleague to become familiar with marking the passage as the child reads.

1. Select a grade-level passage for children to read. Make enough copies so that you have one to mark for each child you evaluate. Either plan to spend a minute in between assessments to do the evaluation, or tape-record the reading of each student so you can review it later.

2. Assess children individually, away from their peers, to ensure privacy and minimize distraction (remember that struggling readers are often embarrassed to read aloud). Make sure the rest of the class is engaged in quiet, independent seat work. Have the child sit next to or across from you, facing away from his or her peers. Position yourself so you can see the other children.

**3.** Encourage the child to read the passage to you as best he or she can. Let the child know that when he or she has finished, you will ask him or her to retell the story.

**4.** Time the child's reading for one minute. On your copy of the passage, put a line through any word the child misses (this includes all mispronunciations, substitutions, and omissions). Do not mark repetitions or hesitations under three seconds. If the child hesitates for three seconds and makes no attempt to read the word, pronounce the word for the child and mark it incorrect. Do not count words the child has added that make sense in context (for example, if in a reading of *Goldilocks and the Three Bears*, a child reads "the bears' house" for "the house," neither count *bears'* as a correct word nor as an error). If a child reads a word incorrectly and then reads the word correctly, write *c* above the word and do not count it as an error. Mark a slash after the last word the child reads when one minute is up.

> Use a stopwatch or kitchen timer to help you focus on children's oral reading without having to watch a clock. Inexpensive kitchen timers may be found at discount and dollar stores.

**5.** Have the child turn the passage facedown. Ask the child to tell you what he or she read, using his or her own words. On the passage, put a check mark in the text over the details the child recalls. For example, if the sentence reads *The three pigs went for a walk*, and the child says, "It's about some pigs who go for a walk," put a check mark over the words *pigs* and *walk*. You may also want to write on the passage the actual words the child says and to jot down any additional information that will be helpful in rating the child's retelling, as shown in the example. For instance, if the child's retelling is in logical order, you might jot down *logical*.

**6.** Thank the child, and provide directions for returning to independent work.

**7.** Immediately following the assessment, or after you have reviewed it with the tape recording later, count the total number of words the child read correctly (wcpm) and rate the quality of the child's oral reading using the Oral Reading Quality Scale on page 108. Rate the child's retelling using the Retelling Comprehension Rubric on page 109. Note the rating scores on the passage and keep the passage in an assessment folder for reference (comparing scored passages taken at different points in the year is a great way to show parents and administrators evidence of a reader's growth).

**8.** Record the child's scores for accuracy, rate, oral reading quality, and retelling on the Fluency Assessment Record (see page 104 for an example).

You may want to do the additional steps listed below once you feel comfortable performing a basic rate and accuracy analysis, as described above. Noting more information from the child's reading will help you to better tailor your instruction.

**I.** Above each word the child misses, write the mispronunciation or substitution the child makes for that word. For example, if in reading the word *house*, the child reads *horse*, write *horse* above the missed word.

**2.** Slash with a diagonal line any part of a word omitted. For example, if the child reads *sun* for *sunshine*, put a line through the word and draw a diagonal line through *shine*.

**3.** As the child reads, mark a slash each time the child pauses after a word or phrase grouping to denote the child's phrasing. You are watching for phrases that are awkwardly grouped and for word-by-word reading.

**4.** Mark an X on any punctuation mark the child omits to indicate that the reader ignores punctuation (this is typical of rapid readers).

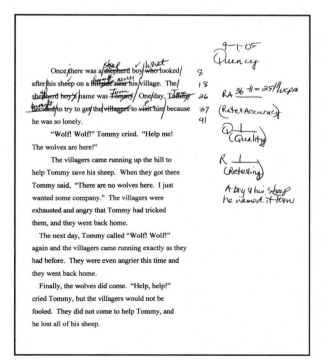

This marked passage shows the results of a second grader's one-minute reading performance taken by his teacher. The assessment shows that Quincy read 36 words with 11 word errors. (Subtract the 11 word errors Quincy made from the 36 total words he read to find his rate: 25 wcpm.) We can see from Quincy's word errors that he missed some basic sight words. He also could not recognize or decode two-syllable words (including the compound word *hillside*) and the three-syllable word *villagers*. Since he read very slowly with a mixture of awkward phrasing and word-by-word reading, he scored 1 out of 4 for oral reading quality. He also scored 1 out of 6 for retelling quality, as he could only correctly recall two details, a boy and the sheep. (Though the section Quincy read was short, the details that he missed in his retelling include the village setting, the boy's name, and what the boy did.)

# *Using Assessment to Guide Instruction*

**B**ased on each child's pre-assessment scores on the Fluency Assessment Record, you'll be able to determine what elements need attention. Then use the chart on page 11 to find strategies that match the needs of each of your readers. Later, based on the growth demonstrated in a midyear assessment, you may wish to focus more intensely on an area where the child needs more support.

In general, readers who need help identifying sight words and sounding out longer words may need to start with activities suggested in the lessons in Chapters 1 and 2. Readers who are having trouble at the sentence level with phrasing may benefit from the activities suggested in Chapter 3. Those who struggle with expression, attending to typographical cues, and retellings may benefit from the activities in Chapter 4. For most struggling readers you may need to apply a combination of techniques from the lessons presented in this book, including repeated readings of texts that support ongoing sight-word recognition, as well as phrasing and expression skills.

At the beginning of the year, Quincy's teacher administered the individual fluency assessments to three struggling readers in her second-grade class. She recorded the data on the Fluency Assessment Record and used this information to determine the fluency instruction she would provide each reader and to decide how she would group them with the other children for instruction.

TEACHER PAGE

## Fluency Assessment Record
### One Minute Timed Oral Reading of Grade-Level Passage

Teacher ___Mrs. Jones_____     Grade __2__     Year_____

| Name | Words Correct Per Minute (Rate and Accuracy) | | | | | | Quality of Oral Reading | | | Retelling Comprehension | | |
|---|---|---|---|---|---|---|---|---|---|---|---|---|
| | Beg Year | % | Mid Year | % | End Year | % | Beg Year | Mid Year | End Year | Beg Year | Mid Year | End Year |
| Quincy | 25/11 | 69 | | | | | | | | | | |
| Larry | 19/10 | 66 | | | | | | | | | | |
| Nan | 46/5 | 90 | | | | | | | | | | |
| | | | | | | | | | | | | |
| | | | | | | | | | | | | |
| | | | | | | | | | | | | |
| | | | | | | | | | | | | |
| | | | | | | | | | | | | |
| | | | | | | | | | | | | |
| | | | | | | | | | | | | |

\* To record the rating number: count the total number of words in the passage and subtract the number of words missed (for example, 100 words read with 3 errors is scored as 97/3).

She found that the oral reading rates of all three of the children were well below the norm of 53 wcpm for second graders at the beginning of the year. She also discovered that the word recognition accuracy of all three of the children was well below the recommended 95 percent, with Quincy and Larry at 69 and 66 percent respectively.

She saw that these two children primarily missed basic sight words and two-syllable words while Nan knew her basic sight words but could not recognize or decode some of the two- and three-syllable words in the text. The children's oral reading quality scores show that all three lack appropriate phrasing and expression when they read aloud. The teacher also found that these assessment results reinforced her own informal observations of the three children's daily reading performance in the classroom.

The teacher's end-of-year goal was to help these children build their fluency to achieve 94 wcpm and to read smoothly with expression and understanding when reading a grade-level passage. She developed a plan to implement word recognition, decoding, and repeated reading strategies each week to increase their skills in reading aloud with accuracy, expression, phrasing, and appropriate rate.

For Quincy and Larry and others in the class with similar needs, the teacher decided to work daily with the Sight-Word Fluency strategy and the Sight-Word Wall Dictionary to build a basic word bank for each reader. To help Nan decode words with two or more syllables, she began with the VIP and Multisyllabic Decoding strategies. (See Chapter 2 for a discussion of these strategies).

To increase the children's phrasing and expression skills, the teacher implemented Dialogue Theater and The Interview Strategy (Chapter 4). She also engaged them in writing and reading their own texts through the use of such strategies as Subject Paragraphs and Individual Experience Stories (Chapter 3).

Since the children's retelling scores indicated they were unable to recall details about what they had read, the teacher also began to use retelling and summarizing strategies after stories the children both heard and read. She also consistently reminded the children, prior to their reading, that they would be responsible for remembering what they had read. She used the retelling rubric to guide and score children's retellings of passages and favorite stories.

"Peer-Assisted Learning Strategies: Promoting Word Recognition, Fluency, and Reading Comprehension in Young Children" by Doug and Lynne Fuchs (*The Journal of Special Education*, 39, 1) is a helpful resource for developing children's retelling and summarizing abilities. It includes best-practice ideas for implementing partner reading and teaching techniques for retelling and summarizing such as "paragraph shrinking."

Ongoing evaluations and a formal midyear assessment will help guide this teacher in determining areas of growth and adjusting the instructional strategies she is now putting into place.

## *Ongoing Assessment*

**A** little assessment at least several times a week helps you make small adjustments to instruction that can scaffold a child's reading growth. Make sure to provide children with opportunities to read aloud every day—to you, with a partner, or in a small guided-reading group. While children are reading, listen for difficulty they may experience with word recognition and decoding, phrasing, and expression. Notice whether their reading rate is too slow or too fast.

As with the formal assessment, use the chart on page 11 to find instructional strategies that will support your readers. For example, a child who has trouble recognizing and decoding key words in a nonfiction reading passage you've reviewed in class needs explicit decoding instruction prior to reading the textbook, followed by multiple opportunities to practice reading the selected passages. (See VIP, pages 30–32; Multisyllabic Decoding, pages 33–35; and Text Chunking, page 36.)

The steps I follow for ongoing fluency assessment for individual readers are:

1. Provide the child a passage for which he or she has learned new vocabulary words through decoding and meaning-based instruction.

2. Observe the child's ability to read aloud the passage—check for an appropriate pace and accurate decoding and note any awkward phrasings or difficulties with expression.

3. Break the text into several manageable chunks and provide the child time to practice repeated readings of the passage with you and a partner.

4. Reassess the child's reading of the passage and record or have the child record his or her rate and accuracy.

5. Ask the child to tell you what the passage is about.

### GETTING READERS INVOLVED

Throughout the year, continue ongoing fluency assessment that encourages your struggling readers to track and record their own progress—and watch themselves grow as readers. If you take regular (weekly) assessments that provide an accuracy/rate score, encourage children, especially older ones, to record their own rate and accuracy on an individual bar graph you have prepared for them. As shown in the example on the next page, you can create a simple graph by writing the rates (in wcpm) on the y-axis from bottom to top. Across the top or bottom of the graph, mark regular intervals for each bar, leaving a space for the child to write the passage name or the date the passage was read. Your students may time each other or you may time them. Have children do at least two timed readings of the passage—one before and the other after they have practiced reading. (Some children may want or need to read the passage more than two times.) Record the results of both on the graph so they can see their progress.

You may find that rates fluctuate due to the content and difficulty of the passages. You may want to explain this to children so they understand why they may see big differences between two consecutive timed reading scores. You might also assign or suggest students use similarly leveled texts each time they test themselves.

I also recommend discussing with children the elements of the Oral Reading Quality Scale, such as appropriate phrasing and expression and actively using these and other fluency terms in your work with struggling readers. The more you use the language of fluency, the more focus and attention you draw to the specific expectations you have of your readers and the more consciously and effectively they can work on skills in those areas. Remember also to include some form of retelling or summarizing as a part of this process to focus children on gaining meaning from the print they are learning to read so fluently.

**Repeated Reading for Fluency Graph**

Student _John D._

| wcpm | Rdg. 1 | Rdg. 2 | Rdg. 1 | Rdg. 2 | Rdg. | Rdg. | Rdg. | Rdg. |
|---|---|---|---|---|---|---|---|---|
| | 9-8 | 9-8 | 9-15 | 9-15 | | | | |
| 95 | | | | | | | | |
| 90 | | | | | | | | |
| 85 | | | | | | | | |
| 80 | | | | | | | | |
| 75 | | | | | | | | |
| 70 | | | | | | | | |
| 65 | | | | | | | | |
| 60 | | | | | | | | |
| 55 | | | | | | | | |
| 50 | | | | | | | | |
| 45 | | | | | | | | |
| 40 | | | | | | | | |
| 35 | | | | | | | | |
| 30 | | | | | | | | |
| 25 | | | | | | | | |
| 20 | | | | | | | | |
| 15 | | | | | | | | |
| 10 | | | | | | | | |
| 5 | | | | | | | | |

Ongoing weekly assessments recorded on fluency graphs and kept by you or your students are a big motivator: They enable you, children, parents, and administrators to see and celebrate progress.

# Oral Reading Quality Scale

**Directions:** Listen to the child read a grade-level passage and rate the quality of reading, using a scale of I to 4. (A score of I or 2 indicates the child exhibits disfluent reading behaviors and needs additional support; a score of 3 or 4 indicates the child is reading with satisfactory to very good fluency.)

| | |
|---|---|
| **4** | **Meaningful phrasing; appropriate rate; engaging expression** |
| **3** | **Appropriate three- to four-word phrasing, rate, and expression** |
| **2** | **Awkward word groupings with some word-by-word phrasing; very slow or fast rate; little or no expression** |
| **I** | **Word-by-word and/or awkward two- to three-word phrasing; very slow rate; no expression**<br><br>**or**<br><br>**Rapid rate; no attention to punctuation or phrasing; little or no expression** |

Adapted from Rasinski, T. V. (2003). "Beyond speed: Reading fluency is more than reading fast." *The California Reader*, 37, 2: 5–11; Rasinski, T. V. (2003). *The Fluent Reader*. New York: Scholastic Inc.

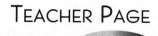

# Retelling Comprehension Rubric

**Directions:** Listen to the child read a grade-level passage, ask the child to retell what he or she has read, and rate the quality of retelling on a scale of 1 to 6. (A score of 1 to 3 indicates that the child has little understanding of what he or she has read and needs support learning to read for understanding and to summarize the reading. A score of 4 indicates the child is able to retain some details but may need help recalling the most important details and putting them in order. A score of 5 or 6 indicates that the child has good to excellent skills in comprehending and summarizing grade-level text.)

| SCORE | QUALITY DESCRIPTOR |
|:-----:|---------------------|
| 6 | **Summarizes the passage in logical order; includes main idea and supporting details; connects to own experiences or other text** |
| 5 | **Summarizes the passage in logical order; includes main idea and supporting details** |
| 4 | **Recalls main idea and a few supporting details in sequence** |
| 3 | **Recalls main idea and a few supporting details out of sequence** |
| 2 | **Recalls several unrelated facts** |
| 1 | **Recalls one or two facts or none** |

Adapted from Rasinski, T. V. (2005). *3-Minute Reading Assessments. Grades 1–4.* New York: Scholastic Inc.

# Fluency Assessment Record
## One-Minute Timed Oral Reading of Grade-Level Passage

Teacher _____  Grade _____  Year _____

| Name | Words Correct Per Minute (Rate and Accuracy) | | | | | | | Quality of Oral Reading | | | Retelling Comprehension | | |
|---|---|---|---|---|---|---|---|---|---|---|---|---|---|
| | Beg Year | % | Mid Year | % | End Year | % | | Beg Year | Mid Year | End Year | Beg Year | Mid Year | End Year |
| | | | | | | | | | | | | | |
| | | | | | | | | | | | | | |
| | | | | | | | | | | | | | |
| | | | | | | | | | | | | | |
| | | | | | | | | | | | | | |
| | | | | | | | | | | | | | |
| | | | | | | | | | | | | | |
| | | | | | | | | | | | | | |
| | | | | | | | | | | | | | |

* To record the rating number: count the total number of words in the passage and subtract the number of words missed (for example, 100 words read with 3 errors is scored as 97/3).

# Dolch Sight-Word List

| | | |
|---|---|---|
| a | been | come |
| about | before | could |
| after | best | cut |
| again | better | did |
| all | big | do |
| always | black | does |
| am | blue | done |
| an | both | don't |
| and | bring | down |
| any | brown | draw |
| are | but | drink |
| around | buy | eat |
| as | by | eight |
| ask | call | every |
| at | came | fall |
| ate | can | far |
| away | carry | fast |
| be | clean | find |
| because | cold | first |

From *Problems in Reading* by Edward William Dolch, Ph.D. (The Garrard Press, 1948).

# Dolch Sight-Word List (continued)

| | | |
|---|---|---|
| five | has | jump |
| fly | have | just |
| for | he | keep |
| found | help | kind |
| four | her | know |
| from | here | laugh |
| full | him | let |
| funny | his | light |
| gave | hold | like |
| get | hot | little |
| give | how | live |
| go | hurt | long |
| goes | I | look |
| going | if | made |
| good | in | make |
| got | into | many |
| green | is | may |
| grow | it | me |
| had | its | much |

From *Problems in Reading* by Edward William Dolch, Ph.D. (The Garrard Press, 1948).

# Dolch Sight-Word List (continued)

| | | |
|---|---|---|
| must | over | seven |
| my | own | shall |
| myself | pick | she |
| never | play | show |
| new | please | sing |
| no | pretty | sit |
| not | pull | six |
| now | put | sleep |
| of | ran | small |
| off | read | so |
| old | red | some |
| on | ride | soon |
| once | right | start |
| one | round | stop |
| only | run | take |
| open | said | tell |
| or | saw | ten |
| our | say | thank |
| out | see | that |

From *Problems in Reading* by Edward William Dolch, Ph.D. (The Garrard Press, 1948).

# Dolch Sight-Word List (continued)

| | | |
|---|---|---|
| the | upon | why |
| their | us | will |
| them | use | wish |
| then | very | with |
| there | walk | work |
| these | want | would |
| they | warm | write |
| think | was | yellow |
| this | wash | yes |
| those | we | you |
| three | well | your |
| to | went | |
| today | were | |
| together | what | |
| too | when | |
| try | where | |
| two | which | |
| under | white | |
| up | who | |

From *Problems in Reading* by Edward William Dolch, Ph.D. (The Garrard Press, 1948).

# Basic Noun List

Add to this list of nouns that you want children to recognize immediately any names of people, places, or things that are specific to your school or town.

| | | |
|---|---|---|
| afternoon | cloud | friend |
| apple | cookie | game |
| aunt | corn | garden |
| baby | country | girl |
| bear | cousin | goodbye |
| bed | cow | grandfather |
| bike | dad | grandmother |
| bird | day | grass |
| birthday | desk | ground |
| boat | dog | hall |
| boy | doll | hill |
| bread | door | home |
| brother | duck | horse |
| bus | evening | house |
| cake | eye | kitten |
| car | family | library |
| cat | farm | light |
| chair | farmer | line |
| chicken | father | lunchroom |
| children | fish | man |
| city | floor | men |
| classroom | flowers | milk |

# Basic Noun List (continued)

| | |
|---|---|
| mom | snow |
| money | song |
| month | squirrel |
| morning | street |
| mother | sun |
| name | table |
| nephew | teacher |
| niece | today |
| night | tomorrow |
| parent | tonight |
| party | truck |
| playground | uncle |
| principal | van |
| puppy | watch |
| rabbit | water |
| rain | way |
| ring | week |
| road | wind |
| room | window |
| school | woman |
| secretary | women |
| sister | wood |
| sleet | year |
| snack | yesterday |

# Suggested Children's Literature for Building Fluency

These are some of the titles I recommend when you use the strategies Teacher Read-Aloud With Multiple Copies, Literature Response Stories, and Dialogue Theater. You will have your favorites to add, too. The asterisks indicate the level of difficulty. Books marked * are appropriate for beginning readers who need practice reading basic sight words in connected text. Books marked ** contain sight words and longer text and are appropriate for children reading at approximately a mid-first-grade level. Books marked *** are picture books containing no text. These books give children opportunities to retell the picture stories orally and in writing. Books not marked are above mid-first-grade level and are most appropriate for use with strategies that target expression and prosody (chapters 3 and 4).

Allard, H. (1977). *Miss Nelson is missing*. Boston, MA: Houghton Mifflin.

*Antle, N. & S. J. (1993). *The good bad cat*. Grand Haven, MI: School Zone Publishing Company.

**Arnold, M. (1996). *Quick, quack, quick*. New York: Random House Children's Books.

Asbjornsen, P. C. (1973). *The three billy goats gruff*. New York: Seabury Press.

Benjamin, C. (1994). *Footprints in the snow*. New York: Scholastic Inc.

Bourgeois, P. (1963). *Franklin in the dark*. New York: Scholastic Inc.

Brett, J. (1990). *Goldilocks and the three bears*. New York: Putnam Juvenile.

Brown, J. (2003). *Flat Stanley*. New York: HarperTrophy.

Bunting, E. (1989). *The Wednesday surprise*. New York: Clarion Books.

# Suggested Children's Literature for Building Fluency (continued)

Burton, V. L. (1943). *Katy and the big snow.* Boston, MA: Houghton Mifflin.

Burton, V. L. (1988). *The little house.* Boston, MA: Houghton Mifflin.

Burton, V. L. (1967). *Mike Mulligan and his steam shovel.* Boston, MA: Houghton Mifflin.

Carle, E. (1994). *The very hungry caterpillar.* New York: Philomel Books.

**Cobb, A. (1996). *Wheels.* New York: Random House Children's Books.

Coerr, E. (1986). *The Josefina story quilt.* New York: Harper & Row.

**Cole, J. (2003). *Norma Jean, jumping bean.* New York: Random House Children's Books.

Cronin, D. (2000). *Click, clack, moo: Cows that type.* New York: Simon & Schuster Children's Publishing.

Daugherty, J. (1938). *Andy and the lion.* New York: Viking Press.

**Eastman, P. D. (1998). *Are you my mother?* New York: Random House Children's Books.

**Eastman, P. D. (2003). *Big dog, little dog.* New York: Beginner Books.

**Edwards, R. (2003). *Five silly fishermen.* New York: Random House Children's Books.

# Suggested Children's Literature for Building Fluency (continued)

Freeman, D. (1968). *Corduroy*. New York: Viking Juvenile.

Galdone, P. (1968). *Bremen Town musicians*. New York: McGraw-Hill.

Galdone, P. (1968). *Henny Penny*. New York: Seabury Press.

Galdone, P. (1972). *The three bears*. New York: Seabury Press.

Galdone, P. (1970). *The three little pigs*. New York: Seabury Press.

**Gelman, R. G. (1992). *More spaghetti, I say!* New York: Scholastic Inc.

**Gerver, J. E. (2001). *The big red sled*. New York: Scholastic Inc.

**Gregorich, B. (1992). *The fox on the box*. Grand Haven, MI: School Zone Publishing Company.

**Gregorich, B. (1992). *I want a pet*. Grand Haven, MI: School Zone Publishing Company.

**Gregorich, B. (1992). *Up went the goat*. Grand Haven, MI: School Zone Publishing Company.

Guilfoile, E. (1957). *Nobody listens to Andrew*. Chicago, IL: Follett Publishing.

Hall, D. (1979). *Ox-cart man*. New York: Viking Press.

**Harrison, D. L. (2003). *Wake up, sun!* New York: Random House Children's Books.

# Suggested Children's Literature for Building Fluency (continued)

*Hillert, M. (1981). *The baby bunny*. Chicago, IL: Follett Publishing Co.

**Hillert, M. (1982). *The boy and the goats*. Chicago, IL: Follett Publishing Co.

*Hillert, M. (1963). *The funny baby*. Chicago, IL: Follett Publishing Co.

*Hillert, M. (1966). *The magic beans*. Chicago, IL: Follett Publishing Co.

*Hillert, M. (1981). *Not I, not I*. Chicago, IL: Follett Publishing Co.

**Hillert, M. (1969). *The snow baby*. Chicago, IL: Follett Publishing Co.

*Hillert, M. (1963). *The three bears*. Chicago, IL: Follett Publishing Co.

*Hillert, M. (1963). *The three little pigs*. Chicago, IL: Follett Publishing Co.

*Hillert, M. (1966). *The yellow boat*. Chicago, IL: Follett Publishing Co.

Hoban, L. (1985). *Arthur's loose tooth*. New York: Harper & Row.

***Hutchins, P. (1968). *Rosie's walk*. New York: Simon & Schuster Children's Publishing.

Keats, E. J. (1996). *The snowy day*. New York: Viking Juvenile.

Keats, E. J. (1998). *Whistle for Willie*. New York: Viking Juvenile.

Kraus, R. (1980). *Leo the late bloomer*. New York: Windmill/Wanderer Books.

# Suggested Children's Literature for Building Fluency (continued)

Leaf, M. (1938). *The story of Ferdinand*. New York: Viking Juvenile.

Lionni, L. (1963). *Swimmy*. New York, Knopf Books for Young Readers.

Lobel, A. (1979). *Days with Frog and Toad*. New York: Harper & Row.

Lobel, A. (1976). *Frog and Toad all year*. New York: Harper & Row.

Lobel, A. (1970). *Frog and Toad are friends*. New York: Harper & Row.

Lobel, A. (1999). *Frog and Toad together*. New York: HarperFestival.

Lobel, A. (1969). *Small pig*. New York: Harper & Row.

MacDonald, M. (1990). *Hedgehog bakes a cake*. New York: Bantam Books for Young Readers.

**Martin, B. (1992). *Brown bear, brown bear, what do you see?* New York: Henry Holt and Co.

***Mayer, M. (1975). *One frog too many*. New York: Dial Press.

McCloskey, R. (1948). *Blueberries for Sal*. New York: Viking Juvenile.

McCloskey, R. (1941). *Make way for ducklings*. New York: Viking Juvenile.

McQueen, L. (1985). *The little red hen*. New York: Scholastic Inc.

Miles, M. (1971). *Annie and the old one*. Boston, MA: Little, Brown.

# Suggested Children's Literature for Building Fluency (continued)

Miller, J. P. (1982). *Little red hen*. New York: Golden Books.

Minarik, E. H. (1968). *A kiss for little bear*. New York: Harper & Row.

Munsch, R. (1980). *The paper bag princess*. Toronto, ON: Annick Press.

Numeroff, L. J. (1995). *If you give a mouse a cookie*. New York: HarperCollins.

O'Connor, J. (1986). *The teeny tiny woman*. New York: Random House Children's Books.

Parish, P. (1999). *Amelia Bedelia*. New York: HarperFestival.

Payne, E. (1944). *Katy no-pocket*. Boston, MA: Houghton Mifflin.

Peet, B. (1962). *Smokey*. Boston, MA: Houghton Mifflin.

**Phillips, J. (2003). *Tiger is a scaredy cat*. New York: Random House Children's Books.

Scieszka, J. (1999). *The true story of the 3 little pigs!* By New York: Viking Juvenile.

Sendak, M. (1963). *Where the wild things are*. New York: Harper & Row.

Silverstein, S. (1964). *The giving tree*. New York: Harper & Row.

Siracusa, C. (1990). *No mail for Mitchell*. New York: Random House Children's Books.

# Suggested Children's Literature for Building Fluency (continued)

Slobodkina, E. (1985). *Caps for sale*. New York: Harper & Row.

Steig, W. (1980). *Sylvester and the magic pebble*. New York: Windmill/Wanderer Books.

Steptoe, J. (1987). *Mufaro's beautiful daughters*. New York: Lothrop, Lee & Shepard Books.

Viorst, J. (1987). *Alexander and the terrible, horrible, no good, very bad day*. New York: Aladdin Paperbacks.

Westcott, N. B. (1987). *Peanut butter and jelly: A play rhyme*. New York: E. P. Dutton.

White, E. B. (1952). *Charlotte's web*. New York: Harper & Row.

Wood, D. & Wood, A. (1990). *The little mouse, the red ripe strawberry, and the big hungry bear*. New York: Child's Play (International).

**Ziefert, H. (2003). *A dozen dogs: A math reader*. New York: Random House Children's Books.

Zion, G. (2002). *Harry the dirty dog*. New York: HarperCollins.

Zion, G. (1999). *Harry and the lady next door*. New York: HarperFestival.

Zion, G. (1958). *No roses for Harry*. New York: Harper & Row.

# Professional Sources Cited

Fuchs, D., & Fuchs, L. S. (2005). Peer-assisted learning strategies: Promoting word recognition, fluency, and reading comprehension in young children. *The Journal of Special Education*, 39 (1), 34–44.

Good, R. H., & Kaminski, R. A. (Eds.). (2002). *Dynamic indicators of basic early literacy skills* (6th ed.). Eugene, OR: Institute for the Development of Educational Achievement. Avail: http://dibels.uoregon.edu/.

Harris, T. L., & Hodges, R. E. (Eds.). (1995). *The literacy dictionary*. Newark, DE: International Reading Association.

Hasbrouck, J. E. & Tindal, G. (1992, Spring). Curriculum-based oral reading fluency forms for students in grades 2 through 5. *Teaching Exceptional Children*, 41–44.

Howe, K. B., & Shinn, M. M. (2001). *Standard reading assessment passages (RAPS) for use in general outcome measurements: A manual describing development and technical features*. Eden Prairie, MN: Edformations.

Kuhn, M. R., & Stahl, S. A. (2000). *Fluency: A review of developmental remedial practices*. Ann Arbor, MI: Center for the Improvement of Early Reading Achievement.

LaBerge, D., & Samuels, S. J. (1974). Toward a theory of automatic information processing in reading. *Cognitive Psychology*, (6), 293–323.

National Reading Panel. (2000). *Report of the national reading panel: Teaching children to read. Report of the subgroups*. Washington, DC: U.S. Department of Health and Human Services, National Institutes of Health. Available: http://www.nichd.nih.gov/publications/nrp/findings.htm.

Opitz, M., & Rasinski, T. V. (1998). *Goodbye round robin*. Portsmouth, NH: Heineman.

Pressley, M. (2002). Comprehension strategies instruction: A turn-of-the-century status report. In C. C. Block & M. Pressley (Eds.), *Comprehension instruction: Research-based best practice*. New York: Guilford Press.

# Professional Sources Cited (continued)

Pressley, M. & Block, C. C. (2002). Summing up. In C. C. Block & M. Pressley (Eds.), *Comprehension instruction: Research-based best practice*. New York: Guilford Press.

Rasinski, T. V. (2003a). Beyond speed: reading fluency is more than reading fast. *California Reader*, (37) 2, 5–11.

Rasinski, T. V. (2003b). *The fluent reader*. New York: Scholastic Professional Books.

Rasinski, T. V., & Padak, N. (2005). *3-minute reading assessments: Word recognition, fluency, and comprehension, Grades 1–4*. New York: Scholastic.

Samuels, J. (1979). The method of repeated readings. *Reading Teacher*, 32, 403–408.

Sinatra, G. M., Brown, K. J., & Reynolds, R. E. (2002). Implications of cognitive resource allocation for comprehension strategies instruction. In C. C. Block & M. Pressley (Eds.), *Comprehension instruction: Research-based best practice*. New York: Guilford Press.

# Children's Literature Cited

Asbjornsen, P. C. (1973). *The three billy goats gruff*. New York: Seabury Press.

Bourgeois, P. (1963). *Franklin in the dark*. New York: Scholastic.

Brown, M. W. (1947). *Goodnight moon*. New York: HarperCollins.

Eastman, P. D. (2003). *Big dog, little dog*. New York: Beginner Books.

Galdone, P. (1970). *The three little pigs*. New York: Seabury Press.

Lobel, A. (1970). *Frog and Toad are friends*. New York: Harper & Row.

McQueen, L. (1985). *The little red hen*. New York: Scholastic Inc.

Piper, W. (1978). *The little engine that could*. New York: Grosset & Dunlap.

Seuss, Dr. (1960). *One fish, two fish, red fish, blue fish*. New York: Random House Books for Young Readers.

Slobodkina, E. (1985). *Caps for sale*. New York: Harper & Row.

White, E. B. (1952). *Charlotte's web*. New York: Harper & Row.

# Index

# Index (continued)